MW00423017

THE
QUOTABLE
CONTRARIAN

THE QUOTABLE CONTЯARIAN

Compiled and Edited by **JAMES JOSEPH**

BlueChip Publishers
Jackson Hole, Wyoming

By nature, quotations are fraught with inaccuracies. It's common to find multiple variations in wording and false attributions. The quotations here are provided in good faith and are accurate to the best of the author's knowledge, but keep in mind the possibility of error. Some quotes may read poorly because they have been left in their original form. Gender pronouns have been left in the form that they're most commonly found, but if appropriate, consider a quote to be gender inclusive.

Copyright © 2021 by James Joseph. All rights reserved.

No part of this book may be reproduced, stored in a retrieval system, or transmitted in any form or by any means, electronic, mechanical, photocopying, recording, or otherwise, without written permission of the publisher, except for the use of brief quotations in a book review.

Printed in the United States of America.

Edited by John Mikeska, Charlie Wilson, and ebooklaunch.com
Cover design by ebooklaunch.com

Print ISBN 978-0-930251-54-3
EPUB ISBN 978-0-930251-57-4
Kindle ISBN 978-0-930251-56-7
PDF ISBN 978-0-930251-55-0

Library of Congress Control Number: 2020911681

BlueChip Publishers
Jackson Hole, Wyoming
BlueChipPublishers.com

Contact the publisher at info@BlueChipPublishers.com
Visit the website for the book at TheQuotableContrarian.com

Available for purchase in bulk and in custom editions.

First edition, version 1.1

CONTENTS

WHAT'S A CONTRARIAN?

Without deviation from the norm, progress is not possible.
— FRANK ZAPPA (1940–1993), ROCK MUSICIAN

A contrarian is someone who rejects popular opinion or opposes the group. A contrarian is unconventional. Contrarian thinking is useful because:

- The crowd is often wrong.
- Creativity and innovation come from thinking differently.
- You can think freely and be yourself.

But sticking your neck out has risks:

- Contrarians are often wrong.
- Contrarians can be annoying.
- Following the crowd is often the best course.
- Not following the crowd is difficult because you become an outsider.

Fortunately, you don't have to be a contrarian to use contrarian thinking. I hope this book inspires you to think critically, to think differently, and to think for yourself.

THE POWER OF A FEW WORDS

> Do you want to sell sugar water for the rest of your life,
> or do you want to come with me and change the world?
> — STEVE JOBS (1955–2011), APPLE COMPUTER

In 1983, that's what Steve Jobs said to John Scully, then president of Pepsi, when Jobs offered Scully the job of Apple president.

A few words can inspire deep thought. A few words can change your way of thinking. A few words can rewire your brain in an instant.

LOOK AT YOURSELF

The first principle is that you must not fool yourself
and you are the easiest person to fool.
— RICHARD FEYNMAN (1918–1988), PHYSICIST

Contrarianism is as much about examining yourself as other people. Look at the arguments you use to validate your thinking. Are they rigorous? Whose path are you on, your own or someone else's?

Idiot Alert: The word *contrarian*, which comes from the root "contra" meaning against, is often used to describe someone who is argumentative. This type of jerk or neckbeard is not who I consider to be a contrarian. Rather, a contrarian is someone who wants to blow the dust off the habitual ways of seeing things.

TIPS AND DISCLAIMERS

Reading a long list of quotations can be tedious. Thumb through and poke around. Try browsing the table of contents for an appealing chapter. Take small bites.

I think Chapter 1, "To Believe in Myths Is Human," is the heart of the book.

Want to engage the contrarian side of your brain? See the last chapter, "Start Asking Questions."

A quote by a particular author is not an endorsement of that person or that person's belief system. The inclusion of an author does not establish that person as a contrarian; it only indicates that the quote fits into a contrarian theme.

Consider that some quotes are by novelists and were spoken by fictional characters. In general, be careful embracing a quote as a battle cry until you discover the context in which it was said.

Some quotes are contradictory. That's the nature of quotations— you pick and choose.

When researching quotes, it's common to find multiple variations in wording and false attributions. I strive for accuracy but in many cases it's impossible to know with 100 percent certainty who said what.

If the exact origin of a quote is uncertain, I note the author as "Unknown" or label it as a "Proverb" or an "Old adage" or something similar.

Some quotes may read poorly because they were taken from informal media, like YouTube or Twitter. I've left quotes in their original form.

Gender rules change over time. I have chosen to leave quotes in the form that they're most commonly found. Please take the quotes in context, and if appropriate, consider them gender inclusive. I apologize if this offends anyone.

If an attribution has no date of death, the author is alive as of the copyright of this book (2021).

Did I leave out your favorite contrarian quote? Please send it my way. I also welcome corrections and feedback:

info@BlueChipPublishers.com

1

TO BELIEVE IN MYTHS IS HUMAN

Believing in myths, stories, and imagined realities may be the most human thing about us. What myths do you believe in?

> A myth is a way of making sense in a senseless world. Myths are narrative patterns that give significance to our existence.
>
> — *Rollo May (1909–1994), psychologist*

> Those who tell the stories rule society.
>
> — *Plato, ancient philosopher*

> We know that people can maintain an unshakable faith in any proposition, however absurd, when they are sustained by a community of like-minded believers.
>
> — *Daniel Kahneman, psychologist and economist*

> All too easily, we confuse the world as we symbolize it with the world as it is.
>
> — *Alan Watts (1915–1973), philosopher*

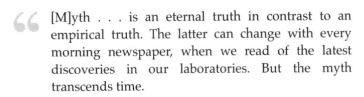

[M]yth . . . is an eternal truth in contrast to an empirical truth. The latter can change with every morning newspaper, when we read of the latest discoveries in our laboratories. But the myth transcends time.

— *Rollo May (1909–1994), psychologist*

How did Homo sapiens manage to cross this critical threshold [of 150 people, which is considered the maximum number of people who can cooperate in an informal group], eventually founding cities comprising tens of thousands of inhabitants and empires ruling hundreds of millions? The secret was probably the appearance of fiction. Large numbers of strangers can cooperate successfully by believing in common myths.

— *Yuval Noah Harari, historian*

Myths which are believed in tend to become true.

— *George Orwell (1903–1950), novelist*

Legends, myths, gods and religions appeared for the first time with the Cognitive Revolution [a shift in thinking and communication 70,000 to 30,000 years ago]. Many animals and human species [other human species that lived alongside *Homo sapiens*] could previously say, 'Careful! A lion!' Thanks to the Cognitive Revolution, *Homo sapiens* acquired the ability to say, 'The lion is the guardian spirit of our tribe.' This ability to speak about fictions is the most unique feature of Sapiens language.

— *Yuval Noah Harari, historian*

Myth fulfills in primitive culture an indispensable function: it expresses, enhances and codifies belief;

it safeguards and enforces morality; it vouches for the efficiency of ritual and contains practical rules for the guidance of man. Myth is thus a vital ingredient of human civilization; it is not an idle tale, but a hard-worked active force; it is not an intellectual explanation or an artistic imagery, but a pragmatic charter of primitive faith and moral wisdom.

— *Bronislaw Kasper Malinowski (1884–1942), anthropologist*

I therefore claim to show, not how men think in myths, but how myths operate in men's minds without their being aware of the fact.

— *Claude Lévi-Strauss (1908–2009), anthropologist*

Most people do not wish to accept that the order governing their lives is imaginary, but in fact every person is born into a pre-existing imagined order, and his or her desires are shaped from birth by its dominant myths.

— *Yuval Noah Harari, historian*

The great enemy of truth is very often not the lie— deliberate, contrived and dishonest—but the myth— persistent, persuasive and unrealistic. Too often we hold fast to the cliches of our forebears. We subject all facts to a prefabricated set of interpretations. We enjoy the comfort of opinion without the discomfort of thought.

— *John F. Kennedy (1917–1963), political leader*

The fact that an opinion has been widely held is no evidence whatever that it is not utterly absurd; indeed in view of the silliness of the majority of mankind, a widespread belief is more likely to be foolish than sensible.

— *Bertrand Russell (1872–1970), philosopher*

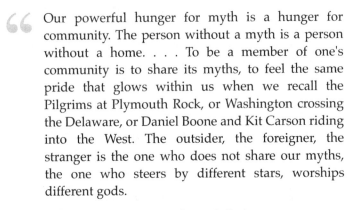 Our powerful hunger for myth is a hunger for community. The person without a myth is a person without a home. . . . To be a member of one's community is to share its myths, to feel the same pride that glows within us when we recall the Pilgrims at Plymouth Rock, or Washington crossing the Delaware, or Daniel Boone and Kit Carson riding into the West. The outsider, the foreigner, the stranger is the one who does not share our myths, the one who steers by different stars, worships different gods.

— *Rollo May (1909–1994), psychologist*

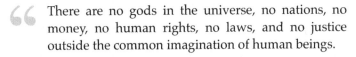 There are no gods in the universe, no nations, no money, no human rights, no laws, and no justice outside the common imagination of human beings.

— *Yuval Noah Harari, historian*

Myth is much more important and true than history. History is just journalism and you know how reliable that is.

— *Joseph Campbell (1904 -1987), writer*

You could never convince a monkey to give you a banana by promising him limitless bananas after death in monkey heaven.

— *Yuval Noah Harari, historian*

2

BELIEVING IS EASIER THAN THINKING

Believing in things is easier than questioning or confronting. Believing in things helps us get through the day.

> For some of our most important beliefs, we have no evidence at all, except that people we love and trust hold these beliefs. Considering how little we know, the confidence we have in our beliefs is preposterous —and it is also essential.
>
> — *Daniel Kahneman, psychologist and economist*

> All belief is fervent hope, and thus a cover-up for doubt and uncertainty.
>
> — *Alan Watts (1915–1973), philosopher*

> There are two ways to be fooled. One is to believe what isn't true; the other is to refuse to believe what is true.
>
> — *Soren Kierkegaard (1813–1855), philosopher*

Believing is easier than thinking. Hence so many more believers than thinkers.

— *Bruce Calvert (1866–1940), publisher*

Every man prefers belief to the exercise of judgment.

— *Seneca, ancient Stoic philosopher*

Faith is much better than belief. Belief is when someone else does the thinking.

— *Buckminster Fuller (1895–1983), architect*

Belief is the death of intelligence. As soon as one believes a doctrine of any sort, or assumes certitude, one stops thinking about that aspect of existence.

— *Robert Anton Wilson (1932–2007), futurist*

Every mental act is composed of doubt and belief, but it is belief that is the positive, it is belief that sustains thought and holds the world together.

— *Soren Kierkegaard (1813–1855), philosopher*

Faith: not wanting to know what is true.

— *Friedrich Nietzsche (1844–1900), philosopher*

A casual stroll through the lunatic asylum shows that faith does not prove anything.

— *Friedrich Nietzsche (1844–1900), philosopher*

Faith is believing in something you know isn't true.

— *Tom Robbins, novelist*

We don't see things as they are; we see them as we are.

— *Unknown*

Most people see what they want to, or at least what they expect to.

— *Martha Grimes, writer*

Man is what he believes.

— *Anton Chekhov (1860–1904), playwright*

If you want to know what your true beliefs are, take a look at your actions.

— *Robert Anthony (1916–2006), organizational theorist*

But once you have a belief system everything that comes in either gets ignored if it doesn't fit the belief system or get[s] distorted enough so that it can fit into the belief system. You gotta be continually revising your map of the world.

— *Robert Anton Wilson (1932–2007), futurist*

Your beliefs can be a prison system created by your mind for yourself. But the door is not locked. If you are aware, you can always come out of that.

— *Amit Ray, writer and spiritual master*

Beliefs are choices. First you choose your beliefs. Then your beliefs affect your choices.

— *Roy T. Bennett, writer*

I have no faith at all. I only hold convictions.

— *Ayn Rand (1905–1982), philosopher*

Nothing is so firmly believed as that which we least know.

— *Michel de Montaigne (1533–1592), writer*

People will believe anything. Except, it seems, the truth.

— *Jeanette Winterson, writer*

Universal opinions are often mistaken for universal principles.

— *Seth Czerepak, writer*

People are embraced or condemned according to their beliefs, so one function of the mind may be to hold beliefs that bring the belief-holder the greatest number of allies, protectors, or disciples, rather than beliefs that are most likely to be true.

— *Steven Pinker, psychologist*

She believed in nothing. Only her skepticism kept her from being an atheist.

— *Jean-Paul Sartre (1905–1980), philosopher*

If you can identify a delusional popular belief, you can find what lies hidden behind it: the contrarian truth.

— *Peter Thiel, internet entrepreneur*

Whenever we hear an opinion and believe it, we make an agreement, and it becomes part of our belief system.

— *Don Miguel Ruiz, writer and spiritual teacher*

What the mind doesn't understand, it worships or fears.

— *Alice Walker, writer*

We have a choice. We have two options as human beings. We have a choice between conversation and war. That's it. Conversation and violence. And faith is a conversation stopper.

— *Sam Harris, neuroscientist*

'You can believe something really hard,' Faith says, 'and still be wrong.'

— *Jodi Picoult, writer*

Belief gets in the way of learning.

— *Robert A. Heinlein (1907–1988), writer*

It is far more comforting to think God listened and said no, than to think that nobody's out there.

— *Mitch Albom, writer*

There's no point in believing in things that exist.

— *Terry Pratchett (1948–2015), writer*

I would rather have a mind opened by wonder than one closed by belief.

— *Gerry Spence, trial lawyer*

Tell people there's an invisible man in the sky who created the universe, and the vast majority will believe you. Tell them the paint is wet, and they have to touch it to be sure.

— *George Carlin (1937–2008), comedian*

3

ON BEING A CONTRARIAN

Contrarians think and rethink. Then they question all the glue that holds the world together.

> It is only because the majority opinion will always be opposed by some that our knowledge and understanding progress.
>
> — *Friedrich Hayek (1899–1992), economist*

> The reasonable man adapts himself to the world: the unreasonable one persists in trying to adapt the world to himself. Therefore all progress depends on the unreasonable man.
>
> — *George Bernard Shaw (1856–1950), playwright*

> A contrarian isn't one who always objects . . . A contrarian reasons independently, from the ground up, and resists pressure to conform.
>
> — *@Naval, Naval Ravikant, internet entrepreneur*

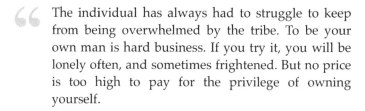

The individual has always had to struggle to keep from being overwhelmed by the tribe. To be your own man is hard business. If you try it, you will be lonely often, and sometimes frightened. But no price is too high to pay for the privilege of owning yourself.

— *Rudyard Kipling (1865–1936), writer*

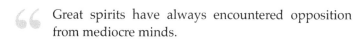

Great spirits have always encountered opposition from mediocre minds.

— *Albert Einstein (1879–1955), physicist*

Follow the path of the unsafe, independent thinker. Expose your ideas to the dangers of controversy. Speak your mind and fear less the label of 'crackpot' than the stigma of conformity. And on issues that seem important to you, stand up and be counted at any cost.

— *Thomas J. Watson (1874–1956), chairman of IBM*

The best opportunities are often ones where you're being contrarian. That doesn't mean being contrarian for contrarian's sake, but it means you're thoughtful about the risks of following the crowd.

— *David Sze, internet entrepreneur*

Contrarian thinking at its best simply asks, *Is that really true?* And it speaks up when the politically correct answer or the conventional wisdom doesn't match reality—when things don't work the way everyone says they do or thinks they do.

— *Larry Osborne, writer and pastor*

You just have to remember that contrarians are usually wrong.

— *Jeff Bezos, Amazon.com*

It's actually pretty easy to be contrarian. It's hard to be contrarian and right.

— *Reid Hoffman, internet entrepreneur*

Cynicism is easy. Mimicry is easy. Optimistic contrarians are the rarest breed.

— *@Naval, Naval Ravikant, internet entrepreneur*

It's very conventional to say that you're a contrarian these days.

— *Reid Hoffman, internet entrepreneur*

When everyone is a contrarian, nobody is a contrarian.

— *Mark Skousen, economist and writer*

I think what's always important is not to be contrarian for its own sake but to really get at the truth.

— *Peter Thiel, internet entrepreneur*

On matters of style, swim with the current. On matters of principle, stand like a rock.

— *Old adage*

Be bold in what you stand for and careful what you fall for.

— *Ruth Boorstin (1917–2013), writer and editor*

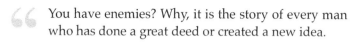

You have enemies? Why, it is the story of every man who has done a great deed or created a new idea.

— *Victor Hugo (1802–1885), poet and novelist*

[John] Adams acknowledged that he had made himself obnoxious to many of his colleagues, who regarded him as a one-man bonfire of the vanities. This never troubled Adams, who in his more contrarian moods claimed that his unpopularity provided clinching evidence that his position was principled, because it was obvious that he was not courting popular opinion. His alienation, therefore, was a measure of his integrity.

— *Joseph J. Ellis, historian*

We have been doing things that are contrary; the things that people tell us won't work from the beginning. In fact, the only way to get ahead is to find errors in conventional wisdom.

— *Larry Ellison, Oracle Corporation*

For it is dangerous to attach one's self to the crowd in front, and so long as each one of us is more willing to trust another than to judge for himself, we never show any judgement in the matter of living, but always a blind trust, and a mistake that has been passed on from hand to hand finally involves us and works our destruction. It is the example of other people that is our undoing; let us merely separate ourselves from the crowd, and we shall be made whole.

— *Seneca, ancient Stoic philosopher*

I am something of a contrarian, I suppose. I feel less comfortable when everybody agrees with me. I say,

'I better reexamine my position!' I probably believe that the worst opinions in my court have been unanimous. Because there's nobody on the other side pointing out all the flaws.

— *Antonin Scalia (1936–2016), supreme court justice*

The most contrarian thing of all is not to oppose the crowd but to think for yourself.

— *Peter Thiel, internet entrepreneur*

Beware the irrational, however seductive. Shun the 'transcendent' and all who invite you to subordinate or annihilate yourself. Distrust compassion; prefer dignity for yourself and others. Don't be afraid to be thought arrogant or selfish. Picture all experts as if they were mammals. Never be a spectator of unfairness or stupidity. Seek out argument and disputation for their own sake; the grave will supply plenty of time for silence. Suspect your own motives, and all excuses. Do not live for others any more than you would expect others to live for you.

— *Christopher Hitchens (1949–2011), writer*

A contrarian at heart, I am often guided by what I disagree with and don't want.

— *Rebecca Solnit, writer*

A society that gets rid of all its troublemakers goes downhill.

— *Robert A. Heinlein (1907–1988), science-fiction writer*

Why do the independent-minded need to be protected, though? Because they have all the new ideas. To be a successful scientist, for example, it's not enough just to be right. You have to be right when everyone else is wrong. Conventional-minded people can't do that. For similar reasons, all successful startup CEOs are not merely independent-minded, but aggressively so. So it's no coincidence that societies prosper only to the extent that they have customs for keeping the conventional-minded at bay.

— *Paul Graham, computer scientist and entrepreneur*

Almost every great achievement began someone finally getting ticked off, saying, 'Enough!' and standing up to fight.

— *Darren Hardy, publisher*

To its devotees the bowtie suggests iconoclasm of an Old World sort, a fusty adherence to a contrarian point of view. The bowtie hints at intellectualism, real or feigned, and sometimes suggests technical acumen, perhaps because it is so hard to tie. Bowties are worn by magicians, country doctors, lawyers and professors and by people hoping to look like the above. But perhaps most of all, wearing a bow tie is a way of broadcasting an aggressive lack of concern for what other people think.

— *Warren St. John, writer*

Whatever it is, I'm against it.

— *Groucho Marx (1890–1977), comedian*

4

THE TRUTH IS PAINFUL

We live in a culture that promotes truth. Yet we believe in so many things that aren't true. The problem with truth is that it often stands in contrast to our beliefs.

> What people believe prevails over the truth.
>
> — *Sophocles, ancient playwright*

> All truth passes through three stages. First, it is ridiculed. Second, it is violently opposed. Third, it is accepted as self-evident.
>
> — *Unknown (often attributed to Schopenhauer)*

> The truth will set you free, but first it will piss you off.
>
> — *Unknown*

> All things are subject to interpretation. Whichever interpretation prevails at a given time is a function of power and not truth.
>
> — *Friedrich Nietzsche (1844–1900), philosopher*

Most men would rather deny a hard truth than face it.

— *George R.R. Martin, writer*

No one is more hated than he who speaks the truth.

— *Plato, ancient philosopher*

You can be standing right in front of the truth and not necessarily see it, and people only get it when they're ready to get it.

— *George Harrison (1943–2001), musician*

I suppose the most revolutionary act one can engage in is . . . to tell the truth.

— *Howard Zinn (1922–2010), historian and activist*

Adversity is the first path to truth.

— *Lord Byron (1788–1824), poet and politician*

Men occasionally stumble over the truth, but most of them pick themselves up and hurry off as if nothing had happened.

— *Winston Churchill (1874–1965), political leader*

We are all capable of believing things which we know to be untrue, and then, when we are finally proved wrong, impudently twisting the facts so as to show that we were right. Intellectually, it is possible to carry on this process for an indefinite time: the only check on it is that sooner or later a false belief bumps up against solid reality, usually on a battlefield.

— *George Orwell (1903–1950), novelist*

Either you repeat the same conventional doctrines everybody is saying, or else you say something true, and it will sound like it's from Neptune.

— *Noam Chomsky, philosopher*

Common sense is not so common.

— *Voltaire (1694–1778), philosopher*

A lie can travel halfway around the world while the truth is putting on its shoes.

— *Unknown*

The further a society drifts from truth, the more it will hate those that speak it.

— *George Orwell (1903–1950), novelist*

The truth is not for all men, but only for those who seek it.

— *Ayn Rand (1905–1982), philosopher*

Rough work, iconoclasm, but the only way to get at truth.

— *Oliver Wendell Holmes Sr. (1809–1894), physician*

The closer you are to the truth, the more silent you become inside.

— *@naval, Naval Ravikant, internet entrepreneur*

Believe those who are seeking the truth. Doubt those who find it.

— *André Gide (1869–1951), writer*

A reliable way to make people believe in falsehoods is frequent repetition, because familiarity is not easily distinguished from truth. Authoritarian institutions and marketers have always known this fact.

— *Daniel Kahneman, psychologist and economist*

Man is least himself when he talks in his own person. Give him a mask, and he will tell you the truth.

— *Oscar Wilde (1854–1900), writer*

The truth is not always beautiful, nor beautiful words the truth.

— *Lao Tzu, ancient Taoist philosopher*

Better a cruel truth than a comfortable delusion.

— *Edward Abbey (1927–1989), environmentalist*

If you would be a real seeker after truth, it is necessary that at least once in your life, you doubt, as far as possible, all things.

— *René Descartes (1596–1650), philosopher*

My way of joking is to tell the truth.

— *George Bernard Shaw (1856–1950), playwright*

If you want to tell people the truth, make them laugh, otherwise they'll kill you.

— *Unknown*

5
_____

THE WISE KNOW NOTHING

People who claim to know much often know the least. And those who know the least are often the most confident. This is the problem with know-it-alls.

> The fool doth think he is wise, but the wise man knows himself to be a fool.
>
> — *William Shakespeare (1564–1616), writer*

> It ain't what you don't know that gets you into trouble. It's what you know for sure that just ain't so.
>
> — *Unknown (often attributed to Mark Twain)*

> The greatest obstacle to discovery is not ignorance— it is the illusion of knowledge.
>
> — *Daniel J. Boorstin (1914–2004), historian*

> No persons are more frequently wrong, than those who will not admit they are wrong.
>
> — *François de La Rochefoucauld (1613–1680), writer*

" A true genius admits that he knows nothing.

— *Albert Einstein (1879–1955), physicist*

" Confidence is ignorance. If you're feeling cocky, it's because there's something you don't know.

— *Eoin Colfer, writer*

" Those who know do not speak. Those who speak do not know.

— *Lao Tzu, ancient Taoist philosopher*

" People tend to hold overly favorable views of their abilities in many social and intellectual domains.... [T]his overestimation occurs, in part, because people who are unskilled in these domains suffer a dual burden: Not only do these people reach erroneous conclusions and make unfortunate choices, but their incompetence robs them of the metacognitive ability to realize it.

— *David Dunning and Justin Kruger, psychologists (this is the cognitive bias known as the "Dunning–Kruger effect")*

" Do not try to seem wise to others.

— *Epictetus, ancient Stoic philosopher*

" A man who knows how little he knows is well; a man who knows how much he knows is sick.

— *Lao Tzu, ancient Taoist philosopher*

" Men cease to think when they think they know it all.

— *Horace, ancient poet*

It is impossible for a man to learn what he thinks he already knows.

— Epictetus, ancient Stoic philosopher

As our circle of knowledge expands, so does the circumference of darkness surrounding it.

— Albert Einstein (1879–1955), physicist

The possession of a strong will and a clever head makes some things very difficult to see.

— Alan Watts (1915–1973), philosopher

The only true wisdom is in knowing you know nothing.

— Socrates, ancient philosopher

We don't know one-millionth of one percent about anything.

— Thomas Edison (1847–1931), inventor

More the knowledge lesser the ego, lesser the knowledge more the ego.

— Albert Einstein (1879–1955), physicist

The most elementary and valuable statement in science, the beginning of wisdom is: I do not know.

— Data, Star Trek: The Next Generation

There are two types of people who lose money: those who know nothing and those who know everything.

— Henry Kaufman, economist

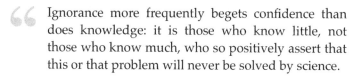

Ignorance more frequently begets confidence than does knowledge: it is those who know little, not those who know much, who so positively assert that this or that problem will never be solved by science.

— *Charles Darwin (1809–1882), naturalist*

One of my most overarching principles is 'knowing how to deal well with what you don't know is much more important than anything you know.'

— *Ray Dalio, investor*

The public have an insatiable curiosity to know everything, except what is worth knowing.

— *Oscar Wilde (1854–1900), writer*

Outside noisy, inside empty.

— *Proverb*

Last year a foolish monk, this year no change.

— *Ryōkan (1758–1831), Zen Buddhist priest*

6

EMBRACE YOUR IGNORANCE

Ignorance can be a path to knowledge. In Zen Buddhism there's a concept called "beginner's mind." It means having an open mind, like the empty and eager mind of a beginner—even if you're at an advanced level.

> In the beginner's mind there are many possibilities, but in the expert's there are few.
>
> — *Shunryu Suzuki (1904–1971), Zen monk*

> We are trying to prove ourselves wrong as quickly as possible, because only in that way can we find progress.
>
> — *Richard Feynman (1918–1988), physicist*

> Our comforting conviction that the world makes sense rests on a secure foundation: our almost unlimited ability to ignore our ignorance.
>
> — *Daniel Kahneman, psychologist and economist*

Whatever inspiration is, it's born from a continuous 'I don't know.'

— *Wislawa Szymborska (1923–2012), poet*

In an honest search for knowledge, you quite often have to abide by ignorance for an indefinite period.

— *Erwin Schrödinger (1887–1961), physicist*

If you wish to improve, be content to appear clueless or stupid in extraneous matters—don't wish to seem knowledgeable. And if some regard you as important, distrust yourself.

— *Epictetus, ancient Stoic philosopher*

Having the confidence to say, 'I don't know' makes you stand out from the crowd. You appear more confident, knowledgeable and ethical despite admitting you don't have all the answers.

— *Lucy King, writer*

To attain knowledge, add things every day. To attain wisdom, subtract things every day.

— *Lao Tzu, ancient Taoist philosopher*

It is what we know already that prevents us from learning.

— *Claude Bernard (1813–1878), physiologist*

The more I learn, the more I realize how much I don't know.

— *Albert Einstein (1879–1955), physicist*

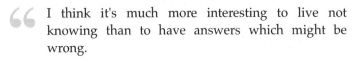

I think it's much more interesting to live not knowing than to have answers which might be wrong.

— *Richard Feynman (1918–1988), physicist*

Ignorance follows knowledge, not the other way around.

— *Stuart Firestein, biologist*

In other words, scientists don't concentrate on what they know, which is considerable but also minuscule, but rather on what they don't know. The one big fact is that science traffics in ignorance, cultivates it, and is driven by it.

— *Stuart Firestein, biologist*

Thoroughly conscious ignorance is the prelude to every real advance in science.

— *James Clerk Maxwell (1831–1879), physicist*

Science is always wrong. It never solves a problem without creating 10 more.

— *George Bernard Shaw (1856–1950), playwright*

Stay hungry. Stay foolish.

— *Steve Jobs (1955–2011), Apple Computer*

7

THE POWER OF DOUBT

How can you be certain that what you know is true? Doubt has its place: it keeps you asking questions.

66 The whole problem with the world is that fools and fanatics are always so certain of themselves, and wiser people so full of doubts.

— *Bertrand Russell (1872–1970), philosopher*

66 Better to trust the man who is frequently in error than the one who is never in doubt.

— *Eric Sevareid (1912–1992), journalist*

66 To doubt everything or to believe everything are two equally convenient solutions; both dispense with the necessity of reflection.

— *Henri Poincaré (1854–1912), mathematician*

66 Certainty is a closing of the mind. To create something new you must have doubt.

— *Milton Glaser, graphic designer*

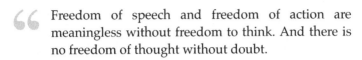

Freedom of speech and freedom of action are meaningless without freedom to think. And there is no freedom of thought without doubt.

— *Bergen Evans (1904–1978), English professor*

Creativity requires the courage to let go of certainties.

— *Erich Fromm (1900–1980), psychoanalyst*

It is the mark of an educated mind to be able to entertain a thought without accepting it.

— *Unknown (often misattributed to Aristotle)*

I am suspicious of all the things that the average people believes.

— *H.L. Mencken (1880–1956), journalist*

Doubt is not a pleasant state of mind, but certainty is absurd.

— *Voltaire (1694–1778), philosopher*

Great intellects are skeptical.

— *Friedrich Nietzsche (1844–1900), philosopher*

The believer is happy; the doubter is wise.

— *Proverb*

I can live with doubt and uncertainty and not knowing. . . . I don't feel frightened by not knowing things, by being lost in the mysterious universe without having any purpose, which is the way it really is, as far as I can tell—possibly.

— *Richard Feynman (1918–1988), physicist*

We all agree that pessimism is a mark of superior intellect.

— *J.K. Galbraith (1908–2006), economist*

I always tell people, pessimists are usually right. Let's face it. Optimists are usually wrong. But all the great change in history, positive change, was done by optimists.

— *Thomas Friedman, journalist*

The power of accurate observation is commonly called cynicism by those who have not got it.

— *George Bernard Shaw (1856–1950), playwright*

It is easier to judge the mind of a man by his questions rather than his answers.

— *Pierre-Marc-Gaston de Lévis (1764–1830), politician and aphorist*

There are no foolish questions, and no man becomes a fool until he has stopped asking questions.

— *Charles Proteus Steinmetz (1865–1923), mathematician and electrical engineer*

I was never aware of any other option but to question everything.

— *Noam Chomsky, philosopher*

Religion is a culture of faith; science is a culture of doubt.

— *Richard Feynman (1918–1988), physicist*

The wise man doesn't give the right answers, he poses the right questions.

— *Claude Lévi-Strauss (1908–2009), anthropologist*

Being a scientist requires having faith in uncertainty, finding pleasure in mystery, and learning to cultivate doubt. There is no surer way to screw up an experiment than to be certain of its outcome.

— *Stuart Firestein, biologist*

'Wait, what?' is first on my list of essential questions because it is an effective way of asking for clarification, and clarification is the first step toward truly understanding something—whether it is an idea, an opinion, a belief, or a business proposal.

— *James E. Ryan, educator and attorney*

Trust, but verify.

— *Proverb (made popular by Ronald Reagan)*

To be absolutely certain about something, one must know everything or nothing about it.

— *Unknown*

Sell your cleverness and buy bewilderment. Cleverness is mere opinion, bewilderment is intuition.

— *Rumi, thirteenth-century poet and mystic*

8

BE CURIOUS

Curiosity is a path to knowledge, understanding, and growth. But a crowd is not curious.

> I have no special talents. I am only passionately curious.
>
> — *Albert Einstein (1879–1955), physicist*

> Satisfaction of one's curiosity is one of the greatest sources of happiness in life.
>
> — *Linus Pauling (1901–1994), chemist*

> I discovered that searching can be as interesting as finding.
>
> — *Paulo Coelho, novelist*

> No one is dumb who is curious. The people who don't ask questions remain clueless throughout their lives.
>
> — *Neil deGrasse Tyson, astrophysicist*

Be a sponge. Curiosity is life. Assumption is death.

— *Mark Parker, former chairman of Nike*

The constant happiness is curiosity.

— *Alice Munro, short story writer*

Curiosity will conquer fear even more than bravery will.

— *James Stephens (1880–1950), poet*

Curiosity is a willing, a proud, an eager confession of ignorance.

— *S. Leonard Rubinstein, author*

By replacing fear of the unknown with curiosity we open ourselves up to an infinite stream of possibility. We can let fear rule our lives or we can become childlike with curiosity, pushing our boundaries, leaping out of our comfort zones, and accepting what life puts before us.

— *Alan Watts (1915–1973), philosopher*

Curiosity is one of the permanent and certain characteristics of a vigorous intellect.

— *Samuel Johnson (1709–1784), writer*

Problems that remain persistently insoluble should always be suspected as questions asked in the wrong way.

— *Alan Watts (1915–1973), philosopher*

Curiosity is the engine of achievement.

— *Sir Kenneth Robinson, writer*

It is a shameful thing to be weary of inquiry when what we search for is excellent.

— *Cicero, ancient philosopher and statesman*

Childhood and genius have the same master-organ in common inquisitiveness.

— *Edwin Bulwer-Lytton (1803–1873), writer*

When people express opinions that differ from yours, take it as a chance to grow. Seek to understand over being understood. Be curious, not defensive. The only way to disarm another human being is by listening.

— *Glennon Doyle Melton, writer*

Why not be curious about why the other person disagrees so profoundly?

— *Michael Jensen, clergyman*

If you are hungry for food, you are prepared to hunt high and low for it. If you are hungry for information it is the same. Information is all around us, now more than ever before in human history. You barely have to stir or incommode yourself to find things out. The only reason people do not know much is because they do not care to know. They are incurious. Incuriosity is the oddest and most foolish failing there is.

— *Stephen Fry, actor*

Millions saw the apple fall, but Newton asked why.

— *Bernard Baruch (1870–1965), financier*

9

INFORMATION AND MISINFORMATION

Most information is "noise." It entertains, distracts and misdirects. It keeps us from thinking straight.

> Facts do not cease to exist because they are ignored.
> — *Aldous Huxley (1894–1963), writer*

> There's a world of difference between truth and facts. Facts can obscure truth.
> — *Maya Angelou (1928–2014), poet*

> There are no facts, only interpretations.
> — *Friedrich Nietzsche (1844–1900), philosopher*

> What information consumes is rather obvious: it consumes the attention of its recipients. Hence a wealth of information creates a poverty of attention.
> — *Herbert A. Simon (1916–2001), economist*

> How it is we have so much information, but know so little?

— *Noam Chomsky, philosopher*

" friendly reminder in times of uncertainty and misinformation: anecdotes are not data. (good) data is carefully measured and collected information based on a range of subject-dependent factors, including, but not limited to, controlled variables, meta-analysis, and randomization

— *@steak_umm, The Steak-Umm Company*

" Like it or not, we're still a primitive tribe ruled by fears, superstition and misinformation.

— *Bill Maher, comedian*

" The Internet commoditized the distribution of facts. The 'news' media responded by pivoting wholesale into opinions and entertainment.

— *@naval, Naval Ravikant, internet entrepreneur*

" Where is the wisdom we have lost in knowledge? Where is the knowledge we have lost in information?

— *T.S. Eliot (1888–1965), poet*

" people think it's bizarre, ironic, and funny when a frozen meat company points out the importance of critical thinking, but chances are the same message would never 'go viral' if it was from a person. our society values entertainment over truth and that's a huge problem

— *@steak_umm, The Steak-Umm Company*

" Democracies die behind closed doors. . . . When government begins closing doors, it selectively controls information rightfully belonging to the people. Selective information is misinformation.

— *Damon Keith (1922–2019), federal judge*

One of the greatest sources of problems in our society arises from people having loads of wrong theories in their heads—often theories that are critical of others—that they won't test by speaking to the relevant people about them. Instead, they talk behind people's backs, which leads to pervasive misinformation.

— *Ray Dalio, investor*

Trust me, Wilbur. People are very gullible. They'll believe anything they see in print.

— *E.B. White (1899–1995), writer*

Until we have a better relationship between private performance and the public truth, as was demonstrated with Watergate, we as the public are absolutely right to remain suspicious, contemptuous even, of the secrecy and the misinformation which is the digest of our news.

— *John le Carré, writer*

I'm very concerned that our society is much more interested in information than wonder. In noise, rather than silence. . . . How do we encourage reflection?

— *Fred Rogers (1928–2003), television host*

What can we do to encourage people to have more quiet in their lives, more silence? Real revelation comes through silence.

— *Fred Rogers (1928–2003), television host*

66 If you repeat a lie often enough, people will believe it. It really is public brainwashing and misinformation.

— *Robert Kane Pappas, filmmaker*

66 What Orwell feared were those who would ban books. What Huxley feared was that there would be no reason to ban a book, for there would be no one who wanted to read one. Orwell feared those who would deprive us of information. Huxley feared those who would give us so much that we would be reduced to passivity and egoism.

— *Neil Postman (1931–2003), writer (comparing George Orwell's* 1984 *with Aldous Huxley's* Brave New World)

66 Take nothing on its looks; take everything on evidence. There is no better rule.

— *Charles Dickens (1812–1970), writer*

66 There are three types of lies—lies, damn lies, and statistics.

— *Unknown*

66 If you torture the data long enough, it will confess to anything.

— *Ronald Coase (1910–2013), economist*

66 To abandon facts is to abandon freedom. If nothing is true, then no one can criticize power, because there is no basis upon which to do so. If nothing is true, then all is spectacle. The biggest wallet pays for the most blinding lights.

— *Timothy Snyder, historian*

Don't cross a river if it is four feet deep on average.

— *Nassim Nicholas Taleb, risk analyst*

Beware of averages. The average person has one breast and one testicle.

— *Dixy Lee Ray (1914–1994), political leader*

10

PROPAGANDA AND BRAINWASHING

People are easy to condition because they want to believe in something. Whether it's advertising or fake news or a politician on the stump, we're easily manipulated.

> The point of modern propaganda isn't only to misinform or push an agenda. It is to exhaust your critical thinking, to annihilate truth.
>
> — *Garry Kasparov, chess master*

> Until you realize how easily it is for your mind to be manipulated, you remain the puppet of someone else's game.
>
> — *Evita Ochel, writer*

> When a well-packaged web of lies has been sold gradually to the masses over generations, the truth will seem utterly preposterous and its speaker a raving lunatic.
>
> — *Dresden James (1931–2008), writer*

Propaganda is as powerful as heroin; it surreptitiously dissolves all capacity to think.

— *Gil Courtemanche (1943–2011), journalist*

One believes things because one has been conditioned to believe them.

— *Aldous Huxley (1894–1963), writer*

Those who can make you believe absurdities can make you commit atrocities.

— *Voltaire (1694–1778), philosopher*

What the advertiser needs to know is not what is right about the product but what is wrong about the buyer.

— *Neil Postman (1931–2003), writer*

If those in charge of our society—politicians, corporate executives, and owners of press and television—can dominate our ideas, they will be secure in their power. They will not need soldiers patrolling the streets. We will control ourselves.

— *Howard Zinn (1922–2010), historian and activist*

The general population doesn't know what's happening, and it doesn't even know that it doesn't know.

— *Noam Chomsky, philosopher*

Political language . . . is designed to make lies sound truthful and murder respectable, and to give an appearance of solidity to pure wind.

— *George Orwell (1903–1950), novelist*

All over the place, from the popular culture to the propaganda system, there is constant pressure to make people feel that they are helpless, that the only role they can have is to ratify decisions and to consume.

— *Noam Chomsky, philosopher*

 The conscious and intelligent manipulation of the organized habits and opinions of the masses is an important element in democratic society. Those who manipulate this unseen mechanism of society constitute an invisible government which is the true ruling power of our country.

We are governed, our minds are molded, our tastes formed, our ideas suggested, largely by men we have never heard of. This is a logical result of the way in which our democratic society is organized. Vast numbers of human beings must cooperate in this manner if they are to live together as a smoothly functioning society. . . .

[I]n almost every act of our daily lives, whether in the sphere of politics or business, in our social conduct or our ethical thinking, we are dominated by the relatively small number of persons . . . who understand the mental processes and social patterns of the masses. It is they who pull the wires which control the public mind.

— *Edward Bernays (1891–1995), pioneer in the field of public relations and propaganda*

 The conformist is not born. He is made. I believe the brainwashing process begins in the schools and colleges.

— *J. Paul Getty (1892–1976), Getty Oil Company*

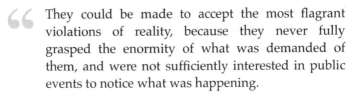 They could be made to accept the most flagrant violations of reality, because they never fully grasped the enormity of what was demanded of them, and were not sufficiently interested in public events to notice what was happening.

— *George Orwell (1903–1950), novelist*

Let's face it. We live in a command-based system, where we have been programmed since our earliest school years to become followers, not individuals. We have been conditioned to embrace teams, the herd, the masses, popular opinion—and to reject what is different, eccentric or stands alone. We are so programmed that all it takes for any business or authority to condition our minds to follow or buy something is to simply repeat a statement more than three or four times until we repeat it ourselves and follow it as truth or the best trendiest thing. This is called 'programming', the frequent repetition of words to condition us how to think, what to like or dislike, and who to follow.

— *Suzy Kassem, filmmaker and poet*

The enormous gap between what U.S. leaders do in the world and what Americans think their leaders are doing is one of the great propaganda accomplishments of the dominant political mythology.

— *Michael Parenti, political scientist*

Alternative facts and fake news are just other names for propaganda.

— *Johnny Corn, comedian*

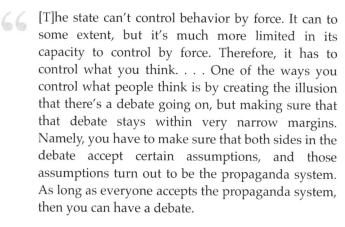

[T]he state can't control behavior by force. It can to some extent, but it's much more limited in its capacity to control by force. Therefore, it has to control what you think. . . . One of the ways you control what people think is by creating the illusion that there's a debate going on, but making sure that that debate stays within very narrow margins. Namely, you have to make sure that both sides in the debate accept certain assumptions, and those assumptions turn out to be the propaganda system. As long as everyone accepts the propaganda system, then you can have a debate.

— *Noam Chomsky, philosopher*

The point of public relations slogans like 'Support our troops' is that they don't mean anything. . . . That's the whole point of good propaganda. You want to create a slogan that nobody's going to be against, and everybody's going to be for. Nobody knows what it means, because it doesn't mean anything. Its crucial value is that it diverts your attention from a question that does mean something: Do you support our policy? That's the one you're not allowed to talk about.

— *Noam Chomsky, philosopher*

just gonna come out and say it: vulnerable people are always the most susceptible to propaganda, misinformation, and conspiracy, especially in times of cultural anxiety, and if there is a way to help them out of these traps, targeted self-righteous vilification isn't it

— *@steak_umm, The Steak-Umm Company*

Only fake people value fake news.

— *Oche Otorkpa, writer*

Today the world is the victim of propaganda because people are not intellectually competent. More than anything the United States needs effective citizens competent to do their own thinking.

— *William Mather Lewis (1878–1945), university president*

Political debate is more interested in manipulating the truth, than finding the truth.

— *George Soros, investor*

We pass our days under the nonstop surveillance of a telescreen that we bought at the Apple Store, carry with us everywhere, and tell everything to, without any coercion by the state. The Ministry of Truth is Facebook, Google, and cable news. We have met Big Brother and he is us.

— *George Packer, journalist (the "Ministry of Truth," which served as a ministry of propaganda, is from George Orwell's book 1984)*

11

BEWARE OF GROUPTHINK

What's one way that experts make mistakes? They follow the crowd.

> [Groupthink is] a mode of thinking that people engage in when they are deeply involved in a cohesive in-group, when the members' strivings for unanimity override their motivation to realistically appraise alternative courses of action.
>
> — *Irving Janis (1918–1990), psychologist (popularized the term* groupthink)

> The main principle of groupthink, which I offer in the spirit of Parkinson's Law, is this: The more amiability and esprit de corps there is among the members of a policy-making in-group, the greater the danger that independent critical thinking will be replaced by groupthink, which is likely to result in irrational and dehumanizing actions directed against outgroups.
>
> — *Irving Janis (1918–1990), psychologist*

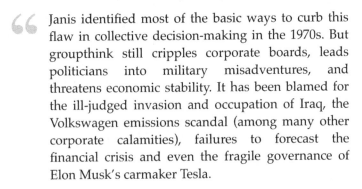 Janis identified most of the basic ways to curb this flaw in collective decision-making in the 1970s. But groupthink still cripples corporate boards, leads politicians into military misadventures, and threatens economic stability. It has been blamed for the ill-judged invasion and occupation of Iraq, the Volkswagen emissions scandal (among many other corporate calamities), failures to forecast the financial crisis and even the fragile governance of Elon Musk's carmaker Tesla.

— *Andrew Hill, journalist and editor*

All of us are not always smarter than one of us, leaders need to distinguish between the wisdom of crowds and the madness of crowds.

— *Paul Gibbons, writer*

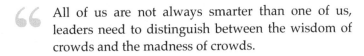 Most of our views are shaped by communal groupthink rather than individual rationality, and we hold on to these views due to group loyalty. Bombarding people with facts and exposing their individual ignorance is likely to backfire. Most people don't like too many facts, and they certainly don't like to feel stupid.

— *Yuval Noah Harari, historian*

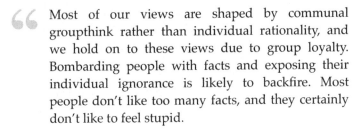 Nor is the people's judgment always true: the most may err as grossly as the few.

— *John Dryden (1631–1700), poet*

Individuals search for truth, groups search for consensus.

— *Naval Ravikant, internet entrepreneur*

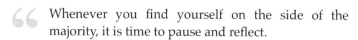 Whenever you find yourself on the side of the majority, it is time to pause and reflect.

— *Mark Twain (1835–1910), humorist*

A group experience takes place on a lower level of consciousness than the experience of an individual. This is due to the fact that, when many people gather together to share one common emotion, the total psyche emerging from the group is below the level of the individual psyche. If it is a very large group, the collective psyche will be more like the psyche of an animal, which is the reason why the ethical attitude of large organizations is always doubtful. The psychology of a large crowd inevitably sinks to the level of mob psychology. If, therefore, I have a so-called collective experience as a member of a group, it takes place on a lower level of consciousness than if I had the experience by myself alone.

— *Carl Jung (1875–1961), psychologist*

[T]he presence of so many people together exerts great suggestive force. The individual in a crowd easily becomes the victim of his own suggestibility. It is only necessary for something to happen, for instance a proposal backed by the whole crowd, and we too are all for it, even if the proposal is immoral. In the crowd one feels no responsibility, but also no fear.

— *Carl Jung (1875–1961), psychologist*

If everyone is thinking alike, then somebody isn't thinking.

— *George S. Patton (1885–1945), army general*

People change when they join crowds. They become more credulous and impulsive, anxiously search for a leader, and react to emotions instead of using their intellect. An individual who becomes involved in a group becomes less capable of thinking for himself.

— *Alexander Elder, psychiatrist and investor*

In fact, the only sin which we never forgive in each other is difference of opinion.

— *Ralph Waldo Emerson (1803–1882), philosopher*

Whenever people agree with me I always feel I must be wrong.

— *Oscar Wilde (1854–1900), writer*

The reasons brainstorming fails are instructive for other forms of group work, too. People in groups tend to sit back and let others do the work; they instinctively mimic others' opinions and lose sight of their own; and, often succumb to peer pressure. The Emory University neuroscientist Gregory Berns found that when we take a stance different from the group's, we activate the amygdala, a small organ in the brain associated with the fear of rejection. Professor Berns calls this the 'pain of independence.'

— *Susan Cain, writer*

If two people always agree, one of them is unnecessary.

— *William Wrigley Jr. (1861–1932), Wrigley's chewing gum*

'Gentlemen, I take it we are all in complete agreement on the decision here.' Everyone around the table nodded assent. 'Then,' continued Mr. Sloan, 'I propose we postpone further discussion of this matter until our next meeting to give ourselves time to develop disagreement and perhaps gain some understanding of what the decision is all about.'

— *Peter F. Drucker (1909–2001), management consultant*

[T]he peculiar evil of silencing the expression of an opinion is, that it is robbing the human race; posterity as well as the existing generation; those who dissent from the opinion, still more than those who hold it. If the opinion is right, they are deprived of the opportunity of exchanging error for truth: if wrong, they lose, what is almost as great a benefit, the clearer perception and livelier impression of truth, produced by its collision with error.

— *John Stuart Mill (1806–1873), philosopher and economist*

[A] well-meaning team of people can sometimes make horrible decisions that no single individual would make. Groupthink, and an unwillingness to disagree with the bosses, was too often a problem at NASA. It may be oversimplifying to say it this way, but in my years as an astronaut, I learned that none of us is as dumb as all of us. That phrase is now clearly posted in the room at NASA used by the Mission Management Team.

— *Mark Kelly, astronaut*

In his classic 1972 book, *Groupthink*, Irving L. Janis, the Yale psychologist, explained how panels of experts could make colossal mistakes. People on these panels, he said, are forever worrying about their personal relevance and effectiveness, and feel that if they deviate too far from the consensus, they will not be given a serious role. They self-censor personal doubts about the emerging group consensus if they cannot express these doubts in a formal way that conforms with apparent assumptions held by the group. . . .

I was connected with the Federal Reserve System as a member [of] the economic advisory panel of the Federal Reserve Bank of New York from 1990 until 2004. . . . In my position on the panel, I felt the need to use restraint. While I warned about the bubbles I believed were developing in the stock and housing markets, I did so very gently, and felt vulnerable expressing such quirky views. Deviating too far from consensus leaves one feeling potentially ostracized from the group, with the risk that one may be terminated.

— *Robert J. Shiller, economist (an excerpt from the* New York Times *in 2008)*

The most important thing in communication is hearing what isn't said.

— *Peter F. Drucker (1909–2001), management consultant*

That which a team does not want to discuss, it most needs to discuss.

— *Paul Gibbons, writer*

People have to learn that consensus is a huge problem. . . . [C]onsensus is how we bully people into pretending that there's nothing to see.

— *Eric Weinstein, mathematician*

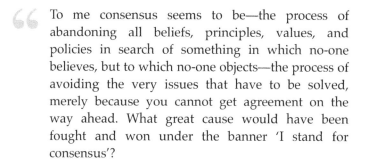 To me consensus seems to be—the process of abandoning all beliefs, principles, values, and policies in search of something in which no-one believes, but to which no-one objects—the process of avoiding the very issues that have to be solved, merely because you cannot get agreement on the way ahead. What great cause would have been fought and won under the banner 'I stand for consensus'?

— *Margaret Thatcher (1925–2013), political leader*

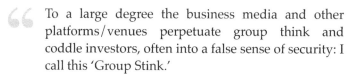 To a large degree the business media and other platforms/venues perpetuate group think and coddle investors, often into a false sense of security: I call this 'Group Stink.'

— *Doug Kass, investor*

12

WHAT COULD GO WRONG?

When considering outcomes, consider bad outcomes. The ancient Stoics had a concept called *negative visualization*. The practice is simple: imagine what could go wrong as a way to prepare yourself for life's inevitable setbacks. It's just a thinking exercise, not a mindset.

> Misfortune weighs most heavily on those who expect nothing but good fortune.
>
> — *Seneca, ancient Stoic philosopher*

> There are downsides to everything; there are unintended consequences to everything.
>
> — *Steve Jobs (1955–2011), Apple Computer*

> Do not indulge in dreams of having what you have not, but reckon up the chief of the blessings you do possess, and then thankfully remember how you would crave for them if they were not yours.
>
> — *Marcus Aurelius, ancient Stoic philosopher*

He robs present ills of their power who has perceived their coming beforehand.

— *Seneca, ancient Stoic philosopher*

Without reflection, we go blindly on our way, creating more unintended consequences, and failing to achieve anything useful.

— *Margaret J. Wheatley, management professor*

[W]e always hear about positive visualization, positive thinking. I think it happens to be overrated and certainly from a pragmatic standpoint, there are times when you have to practice pessimism. Very strategic, tactical, pessimism to get what you want and avoid what you do not want. . . .

[Negative visualization] is all related to the basic assumption that defining your fears, instead of your goals, is a key to doing anything uncommon, anything big. Negative visualization is what I would call preparation in practical pessimism. And that is, defining in excruciating detail the worst case scenarios.

— *Tim Ferriss, writer and internet entrepreneur*

What is quite unlooked for is more crushing in its effect, and unexpectedness adds to the weight of a disaster. The fact that it was unforeseen has never failed to intensify a person's grief. This is a reason for ensuring that nothing ever takes us by surprise. We should project our thoughts ahead of us at every turn and have in mind every possible eventuality instead of only the usual course of events.

— *Seneca, ancient Stoic philosopher*

It is in times of security that the spirit should be preparing itself for difficult times; while fortune is bestowing favors on us then is the time for it to be strengthened against her rebuffs.

— *Seneca, ancient Stoic philosopher*

Hope for the best but expect the worst.

— *Old saying*

[The Stoics] recommended that we spend time imagining that we have lost the things we value— that our wife has left us, our car was stolen, or we lost our job. Doing this, the Stoics thought, will make us value our wife, our car, and our job more than we otherwise would. This technique—let us refer to it as negative visualization—was employed by the Stoics at least as far back as Chrysippus. It is, I think, the single most valuable technique in the Stoics' psychological tool kit.

— *William B. Irvine, philosophy professor*

[I]t is a mistake to think Stoics will spend all their time contemplating potential catastrophes. It is instead something they will do periodically: A few times each day or a few times each week a Stoic will pause in his enjoyment of life to think about how all this, all these things he enjoys, could be taken from him.

Furthermore, there is a difference between contemplating something bad happening and worrying about it. Contemplation is an intellectual exercise, and it is possible for us to conduct such exercises without its affecting our emotions.

— *William B. Irvine, philosophy professor*

About the worst thing that can happen is not something going wrong, but something going wrong and catching you by surprise.

— *Ryan Holiday, writer and media strategist*

There is something wrong with everything.

— *Tyler Cowen, economist*

Confronting the worst-case scenario saps it of much of its anxiety-inducing power. Happiness reached via positive thinking can be fleeting and brittle, negative visualization generates a vastly more dependable calm.

— *Oliver Burkeman, writer*

When you are going to perform an act, remind yourself what kind of things the act may involve. When going to the swimming pool, reflect on what may happen at the pool: some will splash the water, some will push against one another, others will abuse one another, and others will steal. Thusly you have mentally prepared yourself to undertake the act, and you can say to yourself: I now intend to bathe, and am prepared to maintain my will in a virtuous manner, having warned myself of what may occur.

— *Epictetus, ancient Stoic philosopher*

We say that nothing happens to a wise man against his expectation . . . nor do all things turn out for him as he wished but as he reckoned—and above all he reckoned that something could block his plans.

— *Seneca, ancient Stoic philosopher*

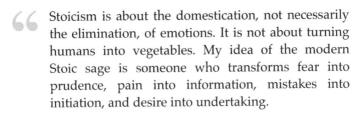 Stoicism is about the domestication, not necessarily the elimination, of emotions. It is not about turning humans into vegetables. My idea of the modern Stoic sage is someone who transforms fear into prudence, pain into information, mistakes into initiation, and desire into undertaking.

— *Nassim Nicholas Taleb, risk analyst*

If you fail to prepare you are preparing to fail.

— *Proverb*

Recent psychological research tends to show that people who are able to accept unpleasant thoughts and feelings, without being overwhelmed by them, are more resilient than people who try to distract themselves or avoid such experiences, through strategies such as positive thinking.

— *Donald Robertson, psychotherapist*

'For Want of a Nail'

For want of a nail the shoe was lost. For want of a shoe the horse was lost. For want of a horse the rider was lost. For want of a rider the message was lost. For want of a message the battle was lost. For want of a battle the kingdom was lost. And all for the want of a horseshoe nail.

— *Proverb*

The word adventure has just gotten overused. For me, adventure is when everything goes wrong. That's when the adventure starts.

— *Yvon Chouinard, rock climber and founder of Patagonia*

13

ARE YOU A CONFORMIST?

Some conformity is necessary to lead an unencumbered life. But too much conformity will extinguish the spark inside of you. When you live in a culture of expectations, thinking differently and speaking out takes courage.

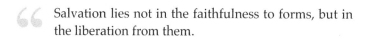 Salvation lies not in the faithfulness to forms, but in the liberation from them.

> — *Boris Pasternak (1890–1960), novelist and poet*

Everybody is identical in their secret unspoken belief that way deep down they are different from everyone else.

> — *David Foster Wallace (1962–2008), writer*

They laugh at me because I'm different; I laugh at them because they're all the same.

> — *Jonathan Davis, musician (often attributed to Kurt Cobain)*

Passivity may be the easy course, but it is hardly the honorable one.

— *Noam Chomsky, philosopher*

The beaten path is the safest but the traffic's terrible.

— *Jeff Taylor, internet entrepreneur*

The opposite to courage is not cowardice. . . The opposite to courage . . . is automaton conformity.

— *Rollo May (1909–1994), psychologist*

Let's start with a test: Do you have any opinions that you would be reluctant to express in front of a group of your peers? If the answer is no, you might want to stop and think about that. If everything you believe is something you're supposed to believe, could that possibly be a coincidence? Odds are it isn't. Odds are you just think what you're told.

— *Paul Graham, computer scientist and entrepreneur*

If you are acting like a sheep, do not blame the shepherd. You cannot herd lions. Wake up and roar and you are free.

— *Papaji (1910–1997), sage*

The mob rushes in where individuals fear to tread.

— *B.F. Skinner (1904–1990), psychologist*

In individuals, insanity is rare; but in groups, parties, nations and epochs, it is the rule.

— *Friedrich Nietzsche (1844–1900), philosopher*

Men, it has been well said, think in herds; it will be seen that they go mad in herds, while they only recover their senses slowly, one by one.

— *Charles MacKay (1814–1889), poet and journalist*

No snowflake in an avalanche ever feels responsible.

— *Stanislaw Jerzy Lec (1909–1966), poet (also attributed to Voltaire)*

A 'collective' mind does not exist. It is merely the sum of endless numbers of individual minds. If we have an endless number of individual minds who are weak, meek, submissive and impotent—who renounce their creative supremacy for the sake of the 'whole' and accept humbly the 'whole's' verdict— we don't get a collective super-brain. We get only the weak, meek, submissive and impotent collective mind.

— *Ayn Rand (1905–1982), philosopher*

Humans are herd animals. We want to fit in, to bond with others, and to earn the respect and approval of our peers. Such inclinations are essential to our survival. For most of our evolutionary history, our ancestors lived in tribes. Becoming separated from the tribe—or worse, being cast out—was a death sentence.

— *James Clear, writer*

In the land of the blind, the one-eyed man will poke out his eye to fit in.

— *Caitlín R. Kiernan, paleontologist*

The first problem of living is to minimize friction with the crowds that surround you on all sides.

— *Isaac Asimov (1920–1992), writer*

We are more wicked together than separately. If you are ever forced to be in a crowd, then most of all you should withdraw into yourself. Never trust another to do your thinking.

— *Jeff Wheeler, writer*

Nature is shy and noncommittal in a crowd. To learn her secrets, visit her alone or with a single friend, at most. Everything evades you, everything hides, even your thoughts escape you, when you walk in a crowd.

— *Edwin Way Teale (1899–1980), naturalist*

None are more hopelessly enslaved than those who falsely believe they are free.

— *Johann Wolfgang von Goethe (1749–1832), writer*

Most people see what they expect to see, what they want to see, what they've been told to see, what conventional wisdom tells them to see–not what is right in front of them in its pristine condition.

— *Vincent Bugliosi (1956–2015), attorney and writer*

Timid men prefer the calm of despotism to the tempestuous sea of liberty.

— *Thomas Jefferson (1743–1826), political leader*

Those who stand for nothing fall for anything.

— *Proverb*

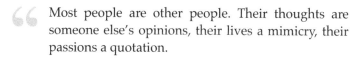

Most people are other people. Their thoughts are someone else's opinions, their lives a mimicry, their passions a quotation.

— *Oscar Wilde (1854–1900), writer*

A foolish consistency is the hobgoblin of little minds, adored by little statesmen and philosophers and divines. With consistency a great soul has simply nothing to do.

— *Ralph Waldo Emerson (1803–1882), philosopher*

Like all men who are fundamentally of the group, of the herd, he was incapable of taking a strong stand with the inevitable loneliness that it implied.

— *F. Scott Fitzgerald (1896–1940), novelist*

We are not supposed to all be the same, feel the same, think the same, and believe the same. The key to continued expansion of our Universe lies in diversity, not in conformity and coercion. Conventionality is the death of creation.

— *Anthon St. Maarten, metaphysical teacher*

I want to stay as close to the edge as I can without going over. Out on the edge you see all kinds of things you can't see from the center. . . . Big, undreamed-of things—the people on the edge see them first.

— *Kurt Vonnegut (1922–2007), writer*

[M]ost people want to believe rather than to know, to take for granted rather than to find out.

— *James Thurber (1894–1961), writer*

No one can possibly achieve any real and lasting success or get rich in business by being a conformist.

— *J. Paul Getty (1892–1976), Getty Oil Company*

Normality is a paved road: It's comfortable to walk, but no flowers grow on it.

— *Vincent van Gogh (1853–1890), artist*

No one ever made a difference by being like everyone else.

— *P.T. Barnum (1810–1891), Barnum & Bailey Circus*

Someday, sometime, you will be sitting somewhere. A berm overlooking a pond in Vermont. The lip of the Grand Canyon at sunset. A seat on the subway. And something bad will have happened: You will have lost someone you loved, or failed at something at which you badly wanted to succeed. And sitting there, you will fall into the center of yourself. You will look for some core to sustain you. And if you have been perfect all your life and have managed to meet all the expectations of your family, your friends, your community, your society, chances are excellent that there will be a black hole where that core ought to be. I don't want anyone I know to take that terrible chance. And the only way to avoid it is to listen to that small voice inside you that tells you to make mischief, to have fun, to be contrarian, to go another way. George Eliot wrote, 'It is never too late to be what you might have been.' It is never too early, either.

— *Anna Quindlen, writer and journalist*

THINK FOR YOURSELF

You have a voice. And you have an inner voice. What is your inner voice saying?

> Don't let the noise of others' opinions drown out your own inner voice.
>
> — *Steve Jobs (1955–2011), Apple Computer*

> The trouble with most people is that they think with their hopes or fears or wishes rather than with their minds.
>
> — *Will Durant (1885–1981), historian*

> Thinking is hard work, which is why you don't see many people doing it.
>
> — *Sue Grafton (1940–2017), mystery writer*

> Clear thinking requires courage rather than intelligence.
>
> — *Thomas Szasz (1920–2012), psychiatrist*

People will come to adore the technologies that undo their capacities to think.

— *Neil Postman (1931–2003), writer*

A sect or party is an elegant incognito devised to save a man from the vexation of thinking.

— *Ralph Waldo Emerson (1803–1882), philosopher*

A contrarian approach is just as foolish as a follow-the-crowd strategy. What is required is thinking rather than polling.

— *Warren Buffett, investor*

Be who you are and say what you feel, because those who mind don't matter and those who matter don't mind.

— *Unknown (often attributed to Dr. Seuss)*

Everything can be taken from a man but one thing: the last of the human freedoms—to choose one's attitude in any given set of circumstances, to choose one's own way.

— *Viktor Frankl (1905–1997), psychiatrist*

Reading, after a certain age, diverts the mind too much from its creative pursuits. Any man who reads too much and uses his own brain too little falls into lazy habits of thinking.

— *Albert Einstein (1879–1955), physicist*

To find yourself, think for yourself.

— *Socrates, ancient philosopher*

People think they are thinking when they are merely rearranging their prejudices.

— *William Fitzjames Oldham (1854–1937), missionary*

A man who does not think for himself does not think at all.

— *Oscar Wilde (1854–1900), writer*

You can forget facts but you cannot forget understanding.

— *Eric Mazur, physicist and educator*

Every pundit who exhorts you to 'think for yourself' really wants you to think like them.

— *Marty Rubin (1930–1994), writer*

Public opinion is a weak tyrant compared with our own private opinion. What a man thinks of himself, that it is which determines, or rather indicates, his fate.

— *Henry David Thoreau (1817–1862), philosopher*

If someone in the street were entrusted with your body, you would be furious. Yet you entrust your mind to anyone around who happens to insult you, and allow it to be troubled and confused. Aren't you ashamed of that?

— *Epictetus, ancient Stoic philosopher*

Thinking for yourself is still a radical act.

— *Nancy Kline, writer*

To go wrong in one's own way is better than to go right in someone else's.

— *Fyodor Dostoevsky (1821–1881), novelist*

The one thing that doesn't abide by majority rule is a person's conscience.

— *Harper Lee (1926–2016), novelist*

The third-rate mind is only happy when it is thinking with the majority. A second-rate mind is only happy when it is thinking with the minority. A first-rate mind is only happy when it is thinking.

— *A.A. Milne (1882–1956), writer*

In questions of science, the authority of a thousand is not worth the humble reasoning of a single individual.

— *Galileo Galilei (1564–1642), astronomer*

Whenever I interview someone for a job, I like to ask this question: 'What important truth do very few people agree with you on?'

This question sounds easy because it's straightforward. Actually, it's very hard to answer. It's intellectually difficult because the knowledge that everyone is taught in school is by definition agreed upon. And it's psychologically difficult because anyone trying to answer must say something she knows to be unpopular. Brilliant thinking is rare. But courage is in even shorter supply than genius.

— *Peter Thiel, internet entrepreneur*

When we blindly adopt a religion, a political system, a literary dogma, we become automatons. We cease to grow.

— *Anaïs Nin (1903–1977), writer*

Someone has said that it requires less mental effort to condemn than to think.

— *Emma Goldman (1869–1940), political activist*

To know what you prefer instead of humbly saying Amen to what the world tells you you ought to prefer, is to have kept your soul alive.

— *Robert Louis Stevenson (1850–1894), writer*

The essence of the independent mind lies not in what it thinks, but in how it thinks.

— *Christopher Hitchens (1949–2011), writer*

Nothing threatens a corrupt system more than a free mind.

— *Suzy Kassem, filmmaker and poet*

The best lightning rod for your protection is your own spine.

— *Ralph Waldo Emerson (1803–1882), philosopher and poet*

You can chain me, you can torture me, you can even destroy this body, but you will never imprison my mind.

— *Mahatma Gandhi (1869–1948), spiritual and political leader*

15

THINK DIFFERENTLY

You don't have to be crazy to have crazy ideas.

> Here's to the crazy ones. The misfits. The rebels. The troublemakers. The round pegs in the square holes. The ones who see things differently. They're not fond of rules. And they have no respect for the status quo. You can quote them, disagree with them, glorify or vilify them. About the only thing you can't do is ignore them. Because they change things. They push the human race forward. And while some may see them as the crazy ones, we see genius. Because the people who are crazy enough to think they can change the world are the ones who do.
>
> — *Apple Computer's "Think Different" advertising campaign (1997)*

> Sometimes it's to your advantage for people to think you're crazy.
>
> — *Thelonious Monk (1917–1982), jazz musician*

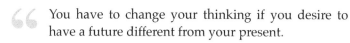

You have to change your thinking if you desire to have a future different from your present.

— *Germany Kent, writer and TV personality*

Instead of thinking outside the box, get rid of the box.

— *Deepak Chopra, alternative-medicine advocate*

The most important thing in science is not so much to obtain new facts as to discover new ways of thinking about them.

— *Sir William Bragg (1890–1971), physicist*

New opinions are always suspected, and usually opposed, without any other reason but because they are not already common.

— *John Locke (1632–1704), philosopher*

If at first the idea is not absurd, then there is no hope for it.

— *Albert Einstein (1879–1955), physicist*

Only one who attempts the absurd is capable of achieving the impossible.

— *Miguel de Unamuno (1864–1936), philosopher*

If we are open only to discoveries which will accord with what we know already, we may as well stay shut.

— *Alan Watts (1915–1973), philosopher*

Practice makes perfect but it doesn't make new.

— *Adam Grant, psychologist*

You have to systematically create confusion, it sets creativity free. Everything that is contradictory creates life.

— *Salvador Dalí (1904–1989), surrealist artist*

If a problem can't be solved within the frame it was conceived, the solution lies in reframing the problem.

— *Brian McGreevy, novelist*

Certainly the revolutionary thinker must go beyond thought. He knows that almost all his best ideas come to him when thinking has stopped. He may have struggled and struggled to understand a problem in terms of old ways of thinking, only to find it impossible. But when thought stops from exhaustion, the mind is open to see the problem as it is—not as it is verbalized—and at once it is understood.

— *Alan Watts (1915–1973), philosopher*

We shouldn't be looking for heroes, we should be looking for good ideas.

— *Noam Chomsky, philosopher*

If we don't believe in freedom of expression for people we despise, we don't believe in it at all.

— *Noam Chomsky, philosopher*

I can't understand why people are frightened of new ideas. I'm frightened of the old ones.

— *John Cage (1912–1992), composer*

16

SECOND-LEVEL THINKING

If you think like everybody else, you will get average results. Consider levels of thinking. *First-level thinking* (also known as *first-order thinking*) is a simple way of thinking that only considers the obvious. *Second-level thinking* is a deeper way of thinking that considers other possibilities.

 First-level thinking is simplistic and superficial and just about everyone can do it. . . . Second-level thinking is deep, complex and convoluted. The second-level thinker takes a great many things into account:

• What is the range of likely future outcomes?

• Which outcome do I think will occur?

• What's the probability I'm right?

• What does the consensus think?

• How does my expectation differ from the consensus?

— *Howard Marks, investor (popularized the phrase* second-level thinking*)*

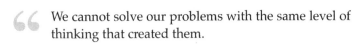

We cannot solve our problems with the same level of thinking that created them.

— *Unknown*

Most people don't do second order thinking because it's hard. It's uncertain. It adds complexity. Second order effects don't fit onto bumper stickers. . . .

More and better second order thinking will serve us well in domains of life, business and government. When we ignore second order effects we end up with grave errors born of our hubris.

— *Noah Pepper, writer*

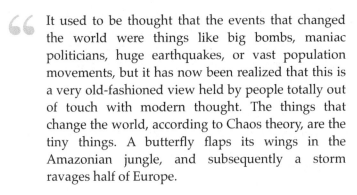

It used to be thought that the events that changed the world were things like big bombs, maniac politicians, huge earthquakes, or vast population movements, but it has now been realized that this is a very old-fashioned view held by people totally out of touch with modern thought. The things that change the world, according to Chaos theory, are the tiny things. A butterfly flaps its wings in the Amazonian jungle, and subsequently a storm ravages half of Europe.

— *Neil Gaiman and Terry Pratchett (1948–2015), writers (an example of the* butterfly effect, *a metaphor for how little things can have big effects)*

Thus, the task is not so much to see what no one yet has seen, but to think what nobody yet has thought about that which everybody sees.

— *Arthur Schopenhauer (1788–1860), philosopher*

Wisdom consists of the anticipation of consequences.

— *Norman Cousins (1915–1990), writer*

 Any endeavor has unintended consequences. Any ill-conceived endeavor has more.

— *Stephen Tobolowsky, actor*

 Multiple level thinking is largely what separates professionals from amateurs [in poker], what separates players who win at the top levels from those who lose. . . .

Simply put, it's the ability to analyze a series of actions on different levels and to use that analysis to formulate likely ranges of hands of your opponents. What are the levels?

[Zeroth level] . . . know what you have, and to know what hands you can beat and what hands beat yours. . . .

[First level] . . . think about what your opponent has. . . .

[Second level] . . . think about what your opponent likely thinks you have. . . .

[Third level] . . . think about what your opponent thinks you think he has. . . .

[Fourth level] . . . think about what your opponent might think that you think he might think you have. . . .

— *David Sklansky and Ed Miller, poker players*

 When we try to pick out anything by itself, we find it hitched to everything else in the Universe.

— *John Muir (1838–1914), naturalist*

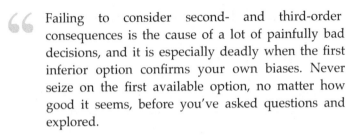 Failing to consider second- and third-order consequences is the cause of a lot of painfully bad decisions, and it is especially deadly when the first inferior option confirms your own biases. Never seize on the first available option, no matter how good it seems, before you've asked questions and explored.

— *Ray Dalio, investor*

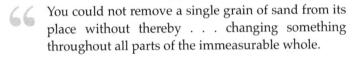 You could not remove a single grain of sand from its place without thereby . . . changing something throughout all parts of the immeasurable whole.

— *Johann Gottlieb Fichte (1762–1814), philosopher*

WALL STREET EMBRACES THE CONTRARIAN

Contrarian investing, popular on Wall Street, is when you go against the market trend. The difficulty with contrarian investing is that you have to go against human nature so most people aren't good at it.

" Buy on the sound of cannons, sell on the sound of trumpets.

— *Nathan Rothschild (1777–1836), financier*

" Buy low, sell high.

— *Old Wall Street saying*

" If you want to have a better performance than the crowd, you must do things differently from the crowd.

— *Sir John Templeton (1912–2008), investor*

" Be fearful when others are greedy and greedy when others are fearful.

— *Warren Buffett, investor*

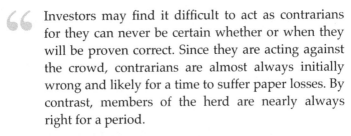

Investors may find it difficult to act as contrarians for they can never be certain whether or when they will be proven correct. Since they are acting against the crowd, contrarians are almost always initially wrong and likely for a time to suffer paper losses. By contrast, members of the herd are nearly always right for a period.

— *Seth Klarman, investor*

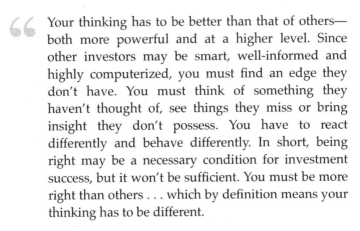

Your thinking has to be better than that of others— both more powerful and at a higher level. Since other investors may be smart, well-informed and highly computerized, you must find an edge they don't have. You must think of something they haven't thought of, see things they miss or bring insight they don't possess. You have to react differently and behave differently. In short, being right may be a necessary condition for investment success, but it won't be sufficient. You must be more right than others . . . which by definition means your thinking has to be different.

— *Howard Marks, investor*

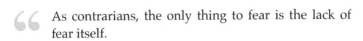

As contrarians, the only thing to fear is the lack of fear itself.

— *Bernie Schaeffer, investor*

Knowing what you don't know is more useful than being brilliant.

— *Charlie Munger, investor*

If everyone is going left, look right.

— *Sam Zell, investor*

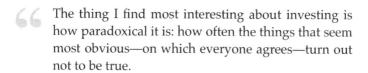

The thing I find most interesting about investing is how paradoxical it is: how often the things that seem most obvious—on which everyone agrees—turn out not to be true.

— *Howard Marks, investor*

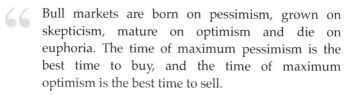

[A]nother thing I have learned in my life is that no matter what we all know today, it's not going to be true in 10 or 15 years. You pick any year in history and go back and then look to see what everybody thought was true in that year, 15 years later the world had changed enormously. Enormously. And yet in that particular year everybody was convinced that this is the way the world was. Pick 1900, 1930, 1950, any year you want to pick, and you will see that 15 years later, the world was totally, totally different from what everybody thought it was at that time.

So I have learned, for whatever reason, to know that change is coming, to know to think against the crowd, that the crowd is nearly always wrong and to try to think for myself. Now, I certainly make plenty of mistakes and have made plenty of mistakes in my life, but these are some of the things that I have learned, to try to think around the corner, try to think to the future if you want to be successful.

— *Jim Rogers, investor*

Bull markets are born on pessimism, grown on skepticism, mature on optimism and die on euphoria. The time of maximum pessimism is the best time to buy, and the time of maximum optimism is the best time to sell.

— *Sir John Templeton (1912–2008), investor*

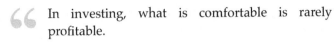 In investing, what is comfortable is rarely profitable.

— *Rob Arnott, investor*

It's not supposed to be easy [investing]. Anyone who finds it easy is stupid.

— *Charlie Munger, investor*

LOOK AT YOUR LIFE THROUGH A CONTRARIAN LENS

You will be influenced and judged by society and the people around you. Staying true to yourself requires conviction and strength. But first it requires introspection.

> So long as men praise you, you can only be sure that you are not yet on your own true path but on someone else's.
>
> — *Friedrich Nietzsche (1844–1900), philosopher*

> If you just set out to be liked, you would be prepared to compromise on anything at any time and you would achieve nothing.
>
> — *Margaret Thatcher (1925–2013), political leader*

> Don't believe everything you think.
>
> — *Unknown*

> That which hinders your task is your task.
>
> — *Sanford Meisner (1905–1997), actor*

Mistakes are the portals of discovery.

— *James Joyce (1882–1941), writer*

Do not seek praise, seek criticism.

— *Paul Arden (1940–2008), creative director*

To avoid criticism, do nothing, say nothing, be nothing.

— *Elbert Hubbard (1856–1915), philosopher*

The greatest deception men suffer is from their own opinions.

— *Leonardo Da Vinci (1452–1519), artist and engineer*

You are under no obligation to remain the same person you were a year ago, a month ago, or even a day ago. You are here to create yourself, continuously.

— *Richard Feynman (1918–1988), physicist*

Begin challenging your own assumptions. Your assumptions are your windows on the world. Scrub them off every once in awhile, or the light won't come in.

— *Alan Alda, actor*

Well it's hard to be yourself, it's the hardest job there is.

— *Bill Murray, actor*

The worst lies are the lies we tell ourselves.

— *Richard Bach, writer*

People reveal much more about themselves while lying.

— *Nassim Nicholas Taleb, risk analyst*

I learned very early the difference between knowing the name of something and knowing something.

— *Richard Feynman (1918–1988), physicist*

When you complain, nobody wants to help you.

— *Stephen Hawking (1942–2018), physicist*

All the suffering there is in this world arises from wishing our self to be happy. All the happiness there is in this world arises from wishing others to be happy.

— *Shantideva, eighth-century Buddhist scholar*

The purpose of life is not to be happy. The purpose of life is to matter, to be productive, to have it make some difference that you lived at all.

— *Leo Rosten (1908–1997), writer*

You probably wouldn't worry about what people think of you if you could know how seldom they do.

— *Olin Miller (1918–2002), writer*

Remembering that you are going to die is the best way I know to avoid the trap of thinking you have something to lose. You are already naked. There is no reason not to follow your heart.

— *Steve Jobs (1955–2011), Apple Computer*

We all get what we tolerate.

— *Tony Robbins, writer and motivational speaker*

" We must be willing to get rid of the life we've planned, so as to have the life that is waiting for us.

— *Joseph Campbell (1904–1987), writer*

" Repetition can be boring or tedious, which is why so few people ever master anything.

— *Hal Elrod, writer*

" Your blessing in life is when you find the torture you're comfortable with.

— *Jerry Seinfeld, comedian*

" You get paid for being right first, and to be first, you can't wait for consensus.

— *@Naval, Naval Ravikant, internet entrepreneur*

" Discipline equals freedom.

— *Jocko Willink, former Navy SEAL commander*

" Great people do things before they're ready. They do things before they know they can do it.

— *Amy Poehler, comedian*

" People who never have any time on their hands are those who do the least.

— *Georg Christoph Lichtenberg (1742–1799), physicist*

" Busy is a decision.

— *Debbie Millman, artist and educator*

Done is better than perfect.

— *Unknown*

Quitting is better than coping because quitting frees you up to excel at something else.

— *Seth Godin, writer*

The time to prepare the roof is when the sun is shining.

— *John F. Kennedy (1917–1963), political leader*

Losers have goals. Winners have systems.

— *Scott Adams, creator of* Dilbert

The greatest of faults . . . is to be conscious of none.

— *Thomas Carlyle (1795–1881), philosopher*

How am I doing?

— *Ed Koch (1924–2013), political leader*

It's easier to act your way into a new way of thinking than think your way into a new way of acting.

— *Unknown*

We are what we repeatedly do. Excellence then, is not an act, but a habit.

— *Will Durant (1885–1981), historian and philosopher*

Deciding what not to do is as important as deciding what to do.

— *Steve Jobs (1955–2011), Apple Computer*

People think focus means saying yes to the thing you've got to focus on. But that's not what it means at all. It means saying no to the hundred other good ideas that there are. You have to pick carefully. I'm actually as proud of the things we haven't done as the things I have done. Innovation is saying no to 1,000 things.

— *Steve Jobs (1955–2011), Apple Computer*

What should I put on my *not*-to-do list?

— *Tim Ferriss, writer and internet entrepreneur*

They think that intelligence is about noticing things that are relevant (detecting patterns); in a complex world, intelligence consists in ignoring things that are irrelevant (avoiding false patterns).

— *Nassim Nicholas Taleb, risk analyst*

The most important aspect of my personality, as far as determining my success goes, has been my questioning conventional wisdom, doubting experts and questioning authority. While that can be painful in your relationships with your parents and teachers, it's enormously useful in life.

— *Larry Ellison, Oracle Corporation*

Progress is impossible without change, and those who cannot change their minds cannot change anything.

— *George Bernard Shaw (1856–1950), playwright*

To improve is to change, so to be perfect is to have changed often.

— *Winston Churchill (1874–1965), political leader*

If someone can prove me wrong and show me my mistake in any thought or action, I shall gladly change. I seek the truth, which never harmed anyone: the harm is to persist in one's own self-deception and ignorance.

— *Marcus Aurelius, ancient Stoic philosopher*

In this world there are only two tragedies. One is not getting what one wants, and the other is getting it.

— *Oscar Wilde (1854–1900), writer*

With advancing age my ideals, which I usually deny possessing, have definitely altered. My ideal is to be free of ideals, free of principles, free of isms and ideologies. I want to take to the ocean of life like a fish takes to the seas. . . . I no longer try to convert people to my view of things, nor to heal them. Neither do I feel superior because they appear to be lacking in intelligence.

— *Henry Miller (1891–1980), writer*

According to Darwin's *Origin of Species*, it is not the most intellectual of the species that survives; it is not the strongest that survives; but the species that survives is the one that is able best to adapt and adjust to the changing environment in which it finds itself.

— *Leon C. Megginson (1921–2010), business professor*

The illiterate of the 21st century will not be those who cannot read and write, but those who cannot learn, unlearn, and relearn.

— *Alvin Toffler (1928–2016), writer and futurist*

It is a sign of weakness to avoid showing signs of weakness.

— *Nassim Nicholas Taleb, risk analyst*

The real journey of discovery consists not of seeking new landscapes, but in having new eyes.

— *Marcel Proust (1871–1922), novelist and critic*

If you don't have an obvious passion, forget about it. Follow your curiosity.

— *Elizabeth Gilbert, writer*

Surrender to your own mediocrity. . . . . I want to write the best novel that has ever been written. . . . . There's this American idea that you reach for those kinds of heights. . . . [T]hat idea of greatness was actually keeping me from fulfilling this dream. . . . . I have to surrender to this notion that even if I'm mediocre, what matters more to me than writing a great novel is writing a novel. That was a huge lesson. . . . I think when we learn that it's not about so much accepting a limitation as accepting that by doing the best work that we have to do, that that's the only way to get to greatness and that we aren't the judge of our own greatness. We're only the judge of our intentions and follow-through.

— *Cheryl Strayed, writer (her answer to Tim Ferriss when asked what she would put on a billboard)*

Eschew the monumental. Shun the epic. All the guys who can paint great big pictures can paint great small ones.

— *Ernest Hemingway (1899–1961), novelist*

Things don't have to change the world to be important.

— *Steve Jobs (1955–2011), Apple Computer*

Be fearful of mediocrity.

— *Jonathan Ellery, artist*

When you grow up, you tend to get told that the world is the way it is. And your life is just to live your life inside the world, try not to bash into the walls too much, try to have a nice family life, have fun, save a little money. But that's a very limited life. Life can be much broader once you discover one simple fact, and that is, everything around you that you call 'life' was made up by people that were no smarter than you, and you can change it, you can influence it, you can build your own things that other people can use. . . . That's maybe the most important thing. It's to shake off this erroneous notion that life is there and you're just going to live in it versus embrace it, change it, improve it, make your mark upon it. . . . Once you learn that you'll never be the same again.

— *Steve Jobs (1955–2011), Apple Computer*

It is not the mountain we conquer, but ourselves.

— *Edmund Hillary (1919–2008), mountain climber*

You are remembered for the rules you break.

— *Douglas MacArthur (1880–1964), army general*

He who dares not offend cannot be honest.

— *Thomas Paine (1737–1809), political philosopher*

Slow is smooth. Smooth is fast.

— *Saying of the Navy SEALs*

Be always restless, unsatisfied, unconforming. Whenever a habit becomes convenient, smash it! The greatest sin of all is satisfaction.

— *Nikos Kazantzakis (1883–1957), writer*

Learn how to learn from those who offend you.

— *Tyler Cowen, economist*

The struggle ends when the gratitude begins.

— *Neale Donald Walsch, spiritual writer*

'Everyone will think it's stupid!'

'Everyone says it's impossible.'

Guess what? Everyone works in the balloon factory and everyone is wrong.

— *Seth Godin, writer*

Enlightenment is ego's ultimate disappointment.

— *Chögyam Trungpa (1939–1987), Buddhist teacher*

You are imperfect, permanently and inevitably flawed. And you are beautiful.

— *Amy Bloom, writer*

The secret of success is sincerity. Once you can fake that you've got it made.

— *Unknown*

19

LESS IS MORE

In a world of temptation, abundance, and the fear of missing out, it's difficult to choose less. In an era of interconnectedness and self-importance, it's difficult to let go. Does choosing more complicate your life?

> A man is rich in proportion to the number of things which he can afford to let alone.

— *Henry David Thoreau (1817–1862), philosopher*

> Learning to ignore things is one of the great paths to inner peace.

— *Robert J. Sawyer, science-fiction writer*

> The height of sophistication is simplicity.

— *Clare Boothe Luce (1903–1987), ambassador*

> Our life is frittered away by detail. . . . Simplicity, simplicity, simplicity!

— *Henry David Thoreau (1817–1862), philosopher*

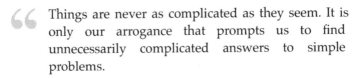

Things are never as complicated as they seem. It is only our arrogance that prompts us to find unnecessarily complicated answers to simple problems.

— *Muhammad Yunus, economist*

The greatest wealth is to live content with little.

— *Plato, ancient philosopher*

Wealth consists not in having great possessions, but in having few wants.

— *Epictetus, ancient Stoic philosopher*

It is not the man who has too little, but the man who craves more, that is poor.

— *Seneca, ancient Stoic philosopher*

It is well worthwhile to go without the things one wants for the greater the sacrifice, the greater the reward when the wish is consummated.

— *Unknown*

He who is not contented with what he has would not be contented with what he would like to have.

— *Unknown (often attributed to Socrates)*

Where there is too much, something is missing

— *Proverb (often attributed to Leo Rosten)*

I should be suspicious of what I want.

— *Rumi, thirteenth-century poet and mystic*

It is not a daily increase, but a daily decrease. Hack away at the inessentials.

— *Bruce Lee (1940–1973), martial artist*

'No' is how you whittle down and sculpt yourself into a work of art. 'Yes' is how [you] burn up and burn out.

— *James Altucher, writer*

Try without trying.

— *Old Zen saying*

There is a Law of Reversed Effort. The harder we try with the conscious will to do something, the less we shall succeed. Proficiency and the results of proficiency come only to those who have learned the paradoxical art of doing and not doing, or combining relaxation with activity, of letting go as a person in order that the immanent and transcendent unknown quantity may take hold. We cannot make ourselves understand; the most we can do is to foster a state of mind, in which understanding may come to us.

— *Aldous Huxley (1894–1963), writer*

I have always been fascinated by the law of reversed effort. Sometimes I call it the 'backwards law.' When you try to stay on the surface of the water, you sink; but when you try to sink, you float. When you hold your breath, you lose it—which immediately calls to mind an ancient and much neglected saying, 'Whosoever would save his soul shall lose it.'

— *Alan Watts (1915–1973), philosopher*

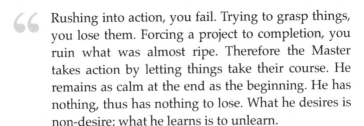

Rushing into action, you fail. Trying to grasp things, you lose them. Forcing a project to completion, you ruin what was almost ripe. Therefore the Master takes action by letting things take their course. He remains as calm at the end as the beginning. He has nothing, thus has nothing to lose. What he desires is non-desire; what he learns is to unlearn.

— *Lao Tzu, ancient Taoist philosopher*

[W]hen you renounce something, you're stuck to it forever. When you fight something, you're tied to it forever. As long as you're fighting it, you are giving it power. You give it as much power as you are using to fight it.

— *Anthony de Mello, writer*

If you worship money and things—if they are where you tap real meaning in life—then you will never have enough. Never feel you have enough. It's the truth. Worship your own body and beauty and sexual allure and you will always feel ugly, and when time and age start showing, you will die a million deaths before they finally plant you. On one level, we all know this stuff already—it's been codified as myths, proverbs, clichés, bromides, epigrams, parables: the skeleton of every great story. The trick is keeping the truth up-front in daily consciousness. Worship power—you will feel weak and afraid, and you will need ever more power over others to keep the fear at bay. Worship your intellect, being seen as smart—you will end up feeling stupid, a fraud, always on the verge of being found out. And so on.

— *David Foster Wallace (1962–2008), writer*

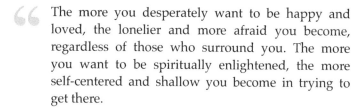 The more you desperately want to be happy and loved, the lonelier and more afraid you become, regardless of those who surround you. The more you want to be spiritually enlightened, the more self-centered and shallow you become in trying to get there.

— *Mark Manson, writer*

Happiness is the absence of the striving for happiness.

— *Chuang Tzu (Zhuangzi), ancient philosopher*

The things you own end up owning you.

— *Chuck Palahniuk, writer*

Talk less and say more.

— *Proverb*

He that loveth silver shall not be satisfied with silver.

— *Ecclesiastes (the Old Testament)*

You may have occasion to possess or use material things, but the secret of life lies in never missing them.

— *Mahatma Gandhi (1869–1948), spiritual and political leader*

I see young men, my townsmen, whose misfortune it is to have inherited farms, houses, barns, cattle, and farming tools; for these are more easily acquired than got rid of.

— *Henry David Thoreau (1817–1862), philosopher*

Many wealthy people are little more than janitors of their possessions.

— *Frank Lloyd Wright (1867–1959), architect*

Attachment is the root of suffering.

— *Buddha, founder of Buddhism*

We live in an age when unnecessary things are our only necessities.

— *Oscar Wilde (1854–1900), writer*

Muddy water is best cleared by leaving it alone.

— *Alan Watts (1915–1973), philosopher*

Manifest plainness, embrace simplicity, reduce selfishness, have few desires.

— *Lao Tzu, ancient Taoist philosopher*

20

EMBRACE FEAR AND HARDSHIP

You would be normal if you wished for an easy life. But growth comes from discontent and adversity.

> Everything you want is just on the other side of fear.
>
> — *Jack Canfield, motivational writer (also attributed to George Addair)*

> Fear makes come true that which one is afraid of.
>
> — *Viktor Frankl (1905–1997), psychiatrist*

> Action cures fear.
>
> — *David J. Schwartz (1927–1987), motivational writer*

> What we fear doing most is usually what we most need to do.
>
> — *Ralph Waldo Emerson (1803–1882), philosopher (also attributed to Tim Ferriss)*

Fear is your friend. It is an indicator. Sometimes it shows you what you shouldn't do, more often than not it shows you what you should do.

— *Tim Ferriss, writer and internet entrepreneur*

Life begins at the end of your comfort zone.

— *Neale Donald Walsch, spiritual writer*

Nothing in life is to be feared, it is only to be understood. Now is the time to understand more, so that we may fear less.

— *Marie Curie (1867–1934), physicist and chemist*

If you don't know, the thing to do is not to get scared, but to learn.

— *Ayn Rand (1905–1982), philosopher*

Fear has its use, but cowardice has none.

— *Mahatma Gandhi (1869–1948), spiritual and political leader*

If it's not scary, everyone else would do it.

— *Ina Garten, cookbook author*

The cave you fear to enter holds the treasure you seek.

—*Joseph Campbell (1904–1987), writer*

The impediment to action advances action. What stands in the way becomes the way.

— *Marcus Aurelius, ancient Stoic philosopher*

Good judgment depends mostly on experience and experience usually comes from poor judgment.

— *Unknown*

 From time to time in the years to come, I hope you will be treated unfairly, so that you will come to know the value of justice. I hope that you will suffer betrayal because that will teach you the importance of loyalty. Sorry to say, but I hope you will be lonely from time to time so that you don't take friends for granted. I wish you bad luck again, from time to time, so that you will be conscious of the role of chance in life and understand that your success is not completely deserved and that the failure of others is not completely deserved either. And when you lose, as you will from time to time, I hope every now and then, your opponent will gloat over your failure. It is a way for you to understand the importance of sportsmanship. I hope you'll be ignored so you know the importance of listening to others, and I hope you will have just enough pain to learn compassion. Whether I wish these things or not, they're going to happen. And whether you benefit from them or not will depend upon your ability to see the message in your misfortunes.

— *John Roberts, supreme court chief justice*

 Everything in life is won through surmounting the associated negative experience. Any attempt to escape the negative, to avoid it or quash it or silence it, only backfires. The avoidance of suffering is a form of suffering. The avoidance of struggle is a struggle. The denial of failure is a failure. Hiding what is shameful is itself a form of shame.

— *Mark Manson, writer*

I have had all of the disadvantages required for success.

— *Larry Ellison, Oracle Corporation*

Comfort makes you weaker. We need some variability, some stressors. Not too much, but just enough.

— *Nassim Nicholas Taleb, risk analyst*

With despair, true optimism begins: the optimism of the man who expects nothing, who knows he has no rights and nothing coming to him, who rejoices in counting on himself alone and in acting alone for the good of all.

— *Jean-Paul Sartre (1905–1980), philosopher*

Never allow a good crisis go to waste. It's an opportunity to do the things you once thought were impossible.

— *Rahm Emanuel, political leader*

Learning is not child's play; we cannot learn without pain.

— *Aristotle, ancient philosopher*

If we are to have intense pleasures, we must also be liable to intense pains.

— *Alan Watts (1915–1973), philosopher*

The wound is the place where the Light enters you.

— *Rumi, thirteenth-century poet and mystic*

21

QUESTION AUTHORITY

When authority rules with a powerful, corrupt, or unjust hand, it breeds discontent. It's the right and the duty of people to speak up.

Blind obedience to authority is the greatest enemy of the truth.

— *Albert Einstein (1879–1955), physicist*

It's frightening to think that you might not know something, but more frightening to think that, by and large, the world is run by people who have faith that they know exactly what's going on.

— *Amos Tversky (1937–1996), psychologist*

War is the health of the state.

— *Randolph Bourne (1886–1918), writer and critic*

Those who make peaceful revolution impossible will make violent revolution inevitable.

— *John F. Kennedy (1917–1963), political leader*

The urge to save humanity is almost always only a false-face for the urge to rule it. Power is what all messiahs really seek: not the chance to serve. This is true even of the pious brethren who carry the gospel to foreign parts.

— *H.L. Mencken (1880–1956), journalist*

If we can but prevent the government from wasting the labours of the people, under the pretence of taking care of them, they must become happy.

— *Thomas Jefferson (1743–1826), political leader*

How do you cause people to believe in an imagined order such as Christianity, democracy or capitalism? First, you never admit that the order is imagined. You always insist that the order sustaining society is an objective reality created by the great gods or by the laws of nature.

— *Yuval Noah Harari, historian*

If you're not going to use your free speech to criticize your own government, then what the hell is the point of having it?

— *Michel Templet, writer*

It could probably be shown by facts and figures that there is no distinctly native American criminal class except Congress.

— *Mark Twain (1835–1910), humorist*

The danger is not that a particular class is unfit to govern. Every class is unfit to govern.

— *Lord Acton (1834–1902), historian*

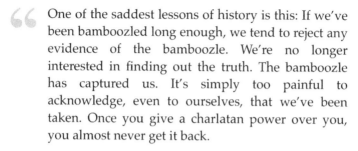

One of the saddest lessons of history is this: If we've been bamboozled long enough, we tend to reject any evidence of the bamboozle. We're no longer interested in finding out the truth. The bamboozle has captured us. It's simply too painful to acknowledge, even to ourselves, that we've been taken. Once you give a charlatan power over you, you almost never get it back.

— *Carl Sagan (1934–1996), astronomer*

When we've got everyone freaked out about staying alive, there's no end to the crazy authoritarian stuff we can get away with. . . . You'll find these ankle monitors to be surprisingly light and comfortable to wear!

— *Ben Hunt, risk analyst*

The worst thing in this world, next to anarchy, is government.

— *Henry Ward Beecher (1813–1887), social reformer*

Many forms of Government have been tried, and will be tried in this world of sin and woe. No one pretends that democracy is perfect or all-wise. Indeed it has been said that democracy is the worst form of Government except for all those other forms that have been tried from time to time.

— *Winston Churchill (1874–1965), political leader*

Relying on the government to protect your privacy is like asking a peeping tom to install your window blinds.

— *John Perry Barlow (1947–2018), lyricist*

I never accept anything about the Government until it has been officially denied; then I know it is true.

— *Unknown*

Democracy is two wolves and a lamb deciding what to have for dinner. Liberty is a well-armed lamb.

— *Unknown (often misattributed to Benjamin Franklin)*

If human beings are fundamentally good, no government is necessary; if they are fundamentally bad, any government, being composed of human beings, would be bad also.

— *Fred Woodworth, publisher*

The whole aim of practical politics is to keep the populace alarmed (and hence clamorous to be led to safety) by menacing it with an endless series of hobgoblins, all of them imaginary.

— *H.L. Mencken (1880–1956), journalist*

The more you can increase fear of drugs and crime, welfare mothers, immigrants and aliens, the more you control all the people.

— *Noam Chomsky, philosopher*

He knows nothing and thinks he knows everything. That points clearly to a political career.

— *George Bernard Shaw (1856–1950), playwright*

Disobedience is the true foundation of liberty.

— *Henry David Thoreau (1817–1862), philosopher*

When the representative body have lost the confidence of their constituents, when they have notoriously made sale of their most valuable rights, when they have assumed to themselves powers which the people never put into their hands, then indeed their continuing in office becomes dangerous to the State, and calls for an exercise of the power of dissolution.

— *Thomas Jefferson (1743–1826), political leader*

It's better to be a pirate than to join the navy.

— *Steve Jobs (1955–2011), Apple Computer*

I don't really know much about pirates, or pirate culture. I'd be a contrarian pirate.

— *Todd Barry, comedian*

No society can exist unless the laws are respected to a certain degree. The safest way to make laws respected is to make them respectable. When law and morality contradict each other, the citizen has the cruel alternative of either losing his moral sense or losing his respect for the law. These two evils are of equal consequence, and it would be difficult for a person to choose between them.

— *Frédéric Bastiat (1801–1850), economist*

There will never be a really free and enlightened State until the State comes to recognize the individual as a higher and independent power, from which all its own power and authority are derived, and treats him accordingly.

— *Henry David Thoreau (1817–1862), philosopher*

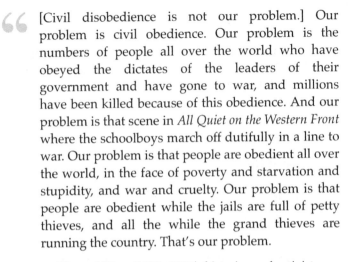

[Civil disobedience is not our problem.] Our problem is civil obedience. Our problem is the numbers of people all over the world who have obeyed the dictates of the leaders of their government and have gone to war, and millions have been killed because of this obedience. And our problem is that scene in *All Quiet on the Western Front* where the schoolboys march off dutifully in a line to war. Our problem is that people are obedient all over the world, in the face of poverty and starvation and stupidity, and war and cruelty. Our problem is that people are obedient while the jails are full of petty thieves, and all the while the grand thieves are running the country. That's our problem.

— *Howard Zinn (1922–2010), historian and activist*

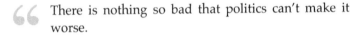

There is nothing so bad that politics can't make it worse.

— *Thomas Sowell, economist*

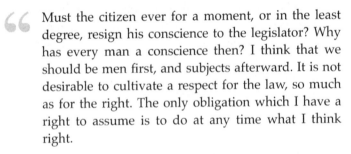

Must the citizen ever for a moment, or in the least degree, resign his conscience to the legislator? Why has every man a conscience then? I think that we should be men first, and subjects afterward. It is not desirable to cultivate a respect for the law, so much as for the right. The only obligation which I have a right to assume is to do at any time what I think right.

— *Henry David Thoreau (1817–1862), philosopher*

The rich man . . . is always sold to the institution which makes him rich.

— *Henry David Thoreau (1817–1862), philosopher*

Every government intervention [in the marketplace] creates unintended consequences, which lead to calls for further government interventions.

— *Ludwig von Mises (1881–1973), economist*

To say that majorities, as such, have a right to rule minorities, is equivalent to saying that minorities have, and ought to have, no rights, except such as majorities please to allow them.

— *Lysander Spooner (1808–1887), legal theorist*

I think it only makes sense to seek out and identify structures of authority, hierarchy, and domination in every aspect of life, and to challenge them; unless a justification for them can be given, they are illegitimate, and should be dismantled, to increase the scope of human freedom.

— *Noam Chomsky, philosopher*

Misguided good men are more dangerous than honest bad men. It is because they are seen as good that, in and by good conscience, the mob will always, stubbornly back them without question.

— *Criss Jami, writer and musician*

No man's life, liberty or property are safe while the legislature is in session.

— *Gideon J. Tucker (1826–1899), judge and politician*

The demagogue is one who preaches doctrines he knows to be untrue to men he knows to be idiots.

— *H.L. Mencken (1880–1956), journalist*

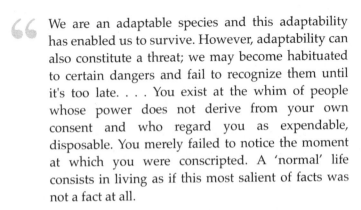

We are an adaptable species and this adaptability has enabled us to survive. However, adaptability can also constitute a threat; we may become habituated to certain dangers and fail to recognize them until it's too late. . . . You exist at the whim of people whose power does not derive from your own consent and who regard you as expendable, disposable. You merely failed to notice the moment at which you were conscripted. A 'normal' life consists in living as if this most salient of facts was not a fact at all.

— *Christopher Hitchens (1949–2011), writer*

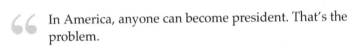

In America, anyone can become president. That's the problem.

— *George Carlin (1937–2008), comedian*

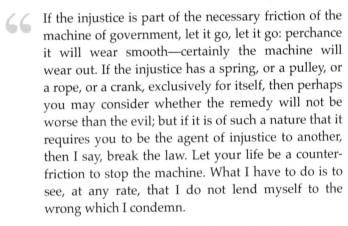

If the injustice is part of the necessary friction of the machine of government, let it go, let it go: perchance it will wear smooth—certainly the machine will wear out. If the injustice has a spring, or a pulley, or a rope, or a crank, exclusively for itself, then perhaps you may consider whether the remedy will not be worse than the evil; but if it is of such a nature that it requires you to be the agent of injustice to another, then I say, break the law. Let your life be a counter-friction to stop the machine. What I have to do is to see, at any rate, that I do not lend myself to the wrong which I condemn.

— *Henry David Thoreau (1817–1862), philosopher*

One has a moral responsibility to disobey unjust laws.

— *Martin Luther King, Jr. (1929–1968), minister*

In the US, there is basically one party—the business party. It has two factions, called Democrats and Republicans, which are somewhat different but carry out variations on the same policies. By and large, I am opposed to these policies. As is most of the population.

— *Noam Chomsky, philosopher*

When I was in high school I asked myself at one point: 'Why do I care if my high school's team wins the football game? I don't know anybody on the team, they have nothing to do with me . . . why am I here and applaud? It does not make any sense.' But the point is, it does make sense: It's a way of building up irrational attitudes of submission to authority and group cohesion behind leadership elements. In fact it's training in irrational jingoism. That's also a feature of competitive sports.

— *Noam Chomsky, philosopher*

To announce that there must be no criticism of the President, or that we are to stand by the President, right or wrong, is not only unpatriotic and servile, but is morally treasonable to the American public.

— *Theodore Roosevelt (1858–1919), political leader*

Authority formally resides 'in the people,' but the power of initiation is in fact held by small circles of men. That is why the standard strategy of manipulation is to make it appear that the people, or at least a large group of them, 'really made the decision.' That is why even when the authority is available, men with access to it may still prefer the secret, quieter ways of manipulation.

— *C. Wright Mills (1916–1962), sociologist*

It is also in the interests of a tyrant to make his subjects poor, so that he may be able to afford the cost of his bodyguard, while the people are so occupied with their daily tasks that they have no time for plotting.

— *Aristotle, ancient philosopher*

Look back over the past, with its changing empires that rose and fell, and you can foresee the future, too.

— *Marcus Aurelius, ancient Stoic philosopher*

Nationalism does nothing but teach you to hate people you've never met. All of a sudden you take pride in accomplishments you had no part in whatsoever.

— *Doug Stanhope, comedian*

Unfortunately, you can't vote the rascals out, because you never voted them in, in the first place.

— *Noam Chomsky, philosopher*

When fascism comes to America, it won't be in brown and black shirts, it won't be with jackboots, it'll be Nike sneakers and smiley shirts.

— *George Carlin (1937–2008), comedian*

Little attention was paid, because the German people, no matter how hungry, remained obedient.

— *Barbara W. Tuchman (1912–1989), historian*

22

KEEP IT REAL

Think for yourself. Question everything. Dismiss habitual ways of thinking. Resist the pressure to conform. Speak up.

> A witty saying proves nothing.
>
> — *Voltaire (1694–1778), philosopher*

> You cannot overestimate the unimportance of practically everything.
>
> — *John C. Maxwell, writer and pastor*

> I think my life is of great importance, but I also think it is meaningless.
>
> — *Albert Camus (1913–1960), philosopher*

> Those are my principles. If you don't like them, I have others.
>
> — *Unknown (often attributed to Groucho Marx)*

START ASKING QUESTIONS

Contrarian thinking can help you find a new perspective or discover the truth. Start by asking questions, of yourself and to the group.

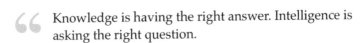 Knowledge is having the right answer. Intelligence is asking the right question.

— *Unknown*

Is it really true? What's the probability that it's true? Is there proof? Could the opposite be true?

Is there more? What if? What then? So what?

Why do you say that? What do you base that on? How certain are you? What's the probability that you're wrong? What could convince you to change your mind? Could we try this instead?

Do I really understand what is being said? How can I think differently about this? What new assumptions can I make to change my way of thinking?

How could the consensus be wrong? What is the probability that the consensus is wrong? What assumptions are the consensus thinkers making? How can I change my way of thinking to outthink the consensus?

What could go wrong? What's the worst that could happen? What's the probability it will happen? What could be the unintended consequences, good and bad? How might things look next year? In five years? How will people respond to this?

Why do I think this way? Why is it important to me? Why do I believe that my way is right? What's the probability that I'm right? How did I come to this conclusion? What are my assumptions and how could they be wrong? Is there a valid counterargument? Is there anything that would make me doubt my belief?

What stories and myths do I believe in? Do I know with 100 percent certainty that these beliefs are true? Do I believe in these stories because it helps me to be accepted by a group? Or because it makes my life easier? Or because I was conditioned to believe them from birth?

 And you're probably not asking the single most important question that can help you achieve a higher level of success and personal fulfillment: How am I doing? This question can be asked in a variety of settings—at work, at home, with friends and colleagues, and even within yourself. The information you gather can be used to set new goals, refine your habits, and generally help you to make the improvements you know you need to make.

— *Jack Canfield, motivational writer*

A Humble 'Ask' from the Author: Did the book make you think? Please write an Amazon review because it helps other people find the book. And it helps me as an author, immensely. I look forward to reading every review.

About the Author

JAMES JOSEPH has been a student of contrarian thinking since 1978, when he put together his first stock portfolio. His inclinations to overthink, ask way too many questions, and flout conventional wisdom have kept him on a contrarian path. Ever cautious of following the herd, he now lives and writes in the mountains of Wyoming.

Acknowledgments

Even a simple book of quotations requires a professional team of skilled editors, artists, and advisors. Thanks to my editors, John Mikeska, Charlie Wilson, and Ebook Launch. Thanks to my cover designer, Ebook Launch. Thanks to my advisors, Bill and Diane Tjenos, Carl Schreier, and Tim Sandlin. And a special thanks to my publishing maven, Ina Stern.